Sisterhood

Sisterhood

Giving and
Receiving the
Gift of
Friendship

CHLOE LANGR

Our Sunday Visitor
Huntington, Indiana

Our Sunday Visitor Publishing Division, Our Sunday Visitor, Inc., 200 Noll Plaza, Huntington, IN 46750; www.osv.com: 1-800-348-2440

ISBN: 978-1-68192-722-0 (Inventory No. T2594)
1. RELIGION—Christian Living—Women's Interests.
2. FAMILY & RELATIONSHIPS—Friendship.
3. RELIGION—Christianity—Catholic.

eISBN: 978-1-68192-723-7
LCCN: 2022930619

Cover and interior design: Lindsey Riesen
Cover and interior art: AdobeStock

PRINTED IN THE UNITED STATES OF AMERICA

To Mary, Hayley, Sarah, and Kelly for receiving my story and giving me the invaluable gift of your friendship.

And to Maeve and Ada — I'm in awe watching your friendship blossom.

In this house, all must be friends, all must be loved, all must be held dear; all must be helped.

— St. Teresa of Ávila

Contents

Contents

Introduction

Do you remember how simple it was to make and keep girlfriends when you were young? All you had to do was wear the same pair of tennis shoes as a classmate and you were set — automatic best friends forever. But the further we are from kindergarten classrooms and recess camaraderie, the more complicated friendships with other women seem to become.

During college, I was blessed with a beautiful group of friends who encountered and accompanied me for four years. For the first time in my life since early grade school, friendships with women were totally joyful and life-giving. But after I graduated from college, my girlfriends weren't just down the street or in the local coffee shops, waiting to share inside jokes and encourage me when I was struggling. Instead, we were spread out throughout the country (and the world!) and weeks, months, and eventually years stretched in between our formerly regular heart-to-heart conversations. The intentionality that friendship requires as an adult hit me like a ton of bricks.

To top it off, I was a transplant in a new city. I was only a few months into the vocation of marriage, settling into a new home, and starting a new job. I often wondered if I would ever be able to make and maintain friendships in this new season of life — I felt like I was in kindergarten all over again. In fact, if I'm being totally honest with you, the idea of having fulfilling, wholesome, and holy sisterhood in that season of life seemed impossible.

While my husband quickly hit it off with long-time college buddies who ended up in the same town after graduation, and fit in seamlessly with our new parish community, I was left with a longing for authentic friendship with women that I just couldn't seem to figure out. I almost started commenting on random strangers' shoes when I stopped in for an espresso at our local coffee spot to see if my old friendship making tricks would pay off again. After all, you can never underestimate the power of a stylish ankle boot to spark a connection. But I was left exhausted. The easy way out seemed to be swearing off establishing new friendships, and just hobbling my friendships from college along, checking in with people every so often despite the miles between us.

Going to events without anyone I knew was so far out of my introverted comfort zone. Small talk was awkward for me, and I never knew quite what to say. While everyone on social media seemed to have their #GirlTribe, I floundered. I burned with jealousy when friends posted pictures of game nights, trips to local wine dives, and girls' vacations that I longed to be included in. I ached for an invitation, to know that someone was thinking of me, remembering me, wanting to invest in a friendship with me. Even though I knew friendship with women could be good, I just wanted to call it quits.

Let's be real: These days, growing in intentional friendship with other women is more challenging than ever. And this follows a broader societal trend, as friendship in general becomes increasingly elusive. Some people today experience a total lack of close friendships in their lives. While our Facebook friend list continues to grow and we connect over the photo grid of Instagram, research finds that two out of five people today admit that their relationships aren't meaningful, and one in five say that they're lonely — defining themselves as socially isolated.[1]

We're facing the irony of being hyperconnected, yet more solitary than ever before. We can list off our friends' breakfasts from their Instagram stories, recall their vacations thanks to Facebook, and laugh at what feel like inside jokes on Twitter. But when was the last time we had an intentional conversation about their day with these same friends, listening to their story instead of watching it on our phones?

As a modern society, our loneliness has reached epidemic levels.[2] But as women, loneliness impacts us in a particular way. Women in all seasons of life report higher levels of loneliness than men.[3] And because we as women tend to focus more on building relationships than men do, a lack of authentic friendship in our lives can leave us wrestling with depression.[4]

Different seasons of life can exacerbate this loneliness. Seasons of singleness, especially when it feels like everyone and their sister is engaged or having babies, can leave you feeling like a very lonely party of one. Yet marriage and motherhood can usher in a different experience of loneliness. Cross-country moves or sharing a calendar with your spouse can make keeping those connections with friends difficult. You might feel alone in your experience of motherhood, exhausted by late nights and early mornings with little people and hungry for an adult conversation about something other than the latest episode of a PBS Kids show. And regardless of your state of life, living through a world pandemic, enduring months of lockdowns, and keeping our physical distance made that ache for friendship and community even more acute.

But physical isolation is not a prerequisite for a desire for deeper, meaningful conversation and communion. Some of us are surrounded by women who we count as friends, but we want to take things to the next level of intentional friendship. How can we patiently navigate the journey from discussions about the weather to heart-to-heart conversations about the big questions in life — and more importantly, how do we know which friends to go deeper with? And when we feel the nudge to take the courageous leap of opening up in healthy vulnerability, how do we resist the urge to smile and claim that everything is "fine" even though we're longing for someone to ask us how we're *really* doing?

We value emotional intimacy with other women. We desire and strive for authentic communication, and work to truly understand the other. In fact, we even go so far as to align and mirror our facial expressions and gestures to the other person's, communicating with our very bodies.[5] But thanks to the sin that has mangled each and every one of our hearts, that good desire for authentic connection and communication also makes our friendships more susceptible to gossip, unhealthy venting, and competition. Maybe you, like me, are all too aware of times in your life where friendships involved comparison, backstabbing, or rejection.

Perhaps, in your own story, you have experienced relationships that lived up to some popular stereotypes surrounding friendship with other women. Maybe a friend made you feel like everything was a competition between the two of you, attempting to one-up you in your successes and finding it difficult to rejoice with you. Or maybe gossip has tainted your interactions, leaving you wondering what your friend said about you when you weren't around. You might be burnt out from friends who left you stranded after they canceled plans with you in favor of something better that came along. Or perhaps you've felt used in past friendships, like you were just the means to someone's end.

Experience with friendships that embodied those tropes or fear of being hurt by them can keep us from trying to form close friendships with women. After all, who needs the drama from *Mean Girls* or *Clueless* in our real lives?

Why not just throw our hands up and walk away from feminine friendships altogether? It seems like an easy option, especially in today's culture which encourages us to embrace independence and autonomy. Or we might be tempted to eschew friendship with other women in favor of friendship with men, which at times can seem simpler and less dramatic.

This isn't to say that you have to be friends with only women. Holy friendship centered in Christ between men and women is possible, and there are amazing examples of saints who strove for a life of virtue alongside the opposite sex in holy friendship centered on Christ — including St. Francis of Assisi and St. Clare of Assisi, Pope St. John Paul II and St. Teresa of Calcutta, and St. Francis de Sales and St. Jane de Chantel. As you examine your friendships while reading this book, many of the topics included here apply to friendship between men and women, too. The truth is that we need each other — despite how messy and broken we all are as human beings. Every single one of us is part of the Body of Christ, and Christ invites us to build each other up in holy, authentic, and healthy friendship.

But here, we're going to focus specifically on feminine friendship because as women, we're especially equipped for this wholesome and holy friendship with the other women in our lives — a friendship that goes beyond the shallow #GirlTribe and achieves true sisterhood.

"Perhaps more than men, women acknowledge the person, because they see persons with their hearts. They see them independently of various ideological or political systems. They see others in their greatness and limitations; they try to go out to them and help them. In this way the basic plan of the Creator takes flesh in the history of humanity and there is constantly revealed, in the variety of vocations, that beauty — not merely physical, but above all spiritual — which God bestowed from the very beginning on all, and in a particular way on women," Saint John Paul wrote in his 1995 *Letter to Women.*

He is speaking to what is perhaps the most incredible aspect of authentic sisterhood. When we are truly present in these friendships, we're able to encounter the beauty that God reveals through the lives of women — and we're able to grow in that beauty ourselves.

But if friendship is so important to not only our lives here on earth, but also our desire for our eternal home, why are so many of us struggling to make and maintain friendships with the women in our lives? One culprit in this struggle is the busyness that rules our daily lives. Friendships take time and intentionality to form, and that's sometimes challenging to order well in the midst of school, family life, and careers. Also, our cultural fascination with technology and social media is impairing our capacity for true friendship with each other. We have hundreds, if not thousands, of connections with women online, but in our hearts we know we're made for deeper intimacy than just responding to stories or clicking "like." And vices like comparison, jealousy, gossip, and pride can get in the way of relationship.

There is a plethora of reasons why we're struggling as women, and unique reasons that answer the *why* in your own story. Servant of God Dorothy Day knew this struggle, too. She wrote about it in her autobiography, *The Long Loneliness.* "I was lonely, deadly lonely. And I was to find out then, as I found out so many times, over and over again, that women especially are social beings, who are not content with just husband and family, but must have community, a group, an exchange with others. Young and old, even in the busiest years of our lives, we women especially are victims of the long loneliness," she reflects. As women, we experience a deep longing for companionship, and the answer to that desire is friendship with other women who inspire us to grow closer to Christ and become the women he's created us to be.

Sisterhood isn't just a trend, or a privilege for a select few of us. Instead, friendship with other women is a necessity for every woman, no matter what season of life we find ourselves in. Each of us longs for the answer to that "long loneliness" we experience in a uniquely feminine way.

The world tells us we need community with other women because those female friendships make us both physically and mentally healthier.[6] Society urges us to look for a shoulder to cry on, a person to boost our self-esteem when we're down, someone to clink wine glasses with in moments of celebration, and women with whom we can gather for a lighthearted brunch with bottomless mimosas on a late Sunday morning. But this mentality encourages us to approach friendship with another woman asking what we can get out of her — which can lead us to believe that friends are people to use so that we can get what we need. But authentic friendship, the kind we need as women and with women, comes from a posture of both receptivity and generosity. We have to start by asking "What do I have to give?" rather than "What can she give me?"

Our relationships with the women in our lives should be occasions for each one of us to build the other up. Instead of being gossip hubs, these friendships should equip us to return to our families and those close to us and love them better. We shouldn't leave conversations with these friends wondering what is said about us after we're out of earshot; these are the friendships that help us bust through those stereotypes of comparison and competition.

Authentic friendship is necessary in our daily lives because *we're made for it*. We're created in the image of a triune God, who is community, communion, and friendship itself. Relationship is stamped into our very spiritual DNA. Not only does God desire to be in relationship with us, he longs for us to be in authentic friendship with others, too. He gives himself as a complete and total gift to us, and asks us to go and do likewise. "If I then, your Lord and Teacher, have washed your feet, you also ought to wash one another's feet," he tells those who follow him. "For I have given you an example, that you also should do as I have done to you." (Jn 13:14–15).

God created you and me as women with a feminine genius. This isn't just a buzzword, or a box that you have to stuff yourself into, or a cookie-cutter model for the one, "perfect" way of living authentically as a Catholic woman. The feminine genius is a phrase. John Paul II used to describe the specific and unique strength of each woman. He recognized that God entrusts humanity to women in a unique way that honors their dignity as daughters of God.

"The hour is coming, in fact, has come, when the vocation of woman is being achieved in its fullness, the hour in which woman acquires in the world an influence, an effect and a power never hitherto achieved. That is why, at this moment when the human race is undergoing so deep a transformation, women impregnated with the spirit of the Gospel can do so much to aid mankind in not falling," he wrote in *Mulieris Dignitatem*.[7] The feminine genius is the way that we as women can keep our entire society on the right path. That's a life-changing truth, and an invitation to freedom, since each woman lives out this unique feminine genius in her own way. You have a beautifully specific way that the Lord is inviting you, asking you, to help the entire human race.

There's a reason that John Paul II thanked every woman for the "simple fact of *being* a woman" when he wrote his *Letter to Women*. Throughout his writings, he mentions four ways that this feminine genius is expressed: receptivity, sensitivity, generosity, and maternity. Those four expressions are incorporated in a wide variety of qualities and characteristics. Every woman, regardless of her state in life or her vocation, is called to live the feminine genius in her own beautifully unrepeatable way. We live it out in our roles as daughters, sisters, mothers, coworkers, and friends, through our conversations, interactions, reflections, and daily life.

Regardless of your state of life, there is one thing that holds true for each one of us as we discover what it means to live fully alive: We have to unpack and explore our feminine genius with the women in our lives. In relationships with our mothers, sisters, friends, daughters, and neighbors, we see true femininity modeled. In conversation with them, we discover truths about who we are and who God is. Those same women remind us what is truly important each day as we strive for lasting joy and holiness.

We don't need a #GirlTribe — but we do need sisterhood in order to flourish! "Friendship is a thing most necessary to life, since without friends no one would choose to live, though possessed of all other advantages," Aristotle famously penned all those years ago. Despite the centuries between those of us here today and Aristotle, his wisdom still rings true in our daily lives. We need sisterhood, even when it's awkward, hard, challenging, or seemingly impossible. No, *especially* then.

Because in those moments, we can begin to realize what a gift friendship is: one that we not only give, but also receive. And when we are able to understand friendship as a gift, we can give ourselves and receive other women in a way we never have before. We can grow in authentic friendship in ways we never thought were possible.

"Dare to love and to be a real friend. The love you give and receive is a reality that will lead you closer and closer to God as well as those whom God has given you to love," writes Henri Nouwen, a Catholic priest, professor, writer, and theologian.

The love you give and receive. The gift of friendship is not just something that you give to other women, but it's something you receive in turn, as well. And not only that, but the very gift of sisterhood is a gift from God. I'm not an expert when it comes to giving and receiving the gift of feminine friendship in my own life — my first few years after college are proof of that. As the years have passed, I'm now blessed both with a new community of women I have settled into, and also the rekindling of friendships from past seasons. I've learned so much about friendship, the Lord, and my own heart in intentional conversations in small groups, coffee shops chasing toddlers, and on phone calls with friends who may live a hundred miles away, but are still very much a part of my life as a Catholic woman.

But I know there is still so much I need to learn about friendships with women in my life. Sometimes during the writing process of this book, I wondered if the reason God invited me into this project was because he wanted me to learn more about the art of friendship myself. But the beauty of recognizing friendship as a gift is that we can always become better at giving ourselves to the other — and we can always grow in the art of receiving the gift of others, too.

I invite you to learn about the gift of friendship with me. In these pages, we'll explore what it means to be a Eucharistic friend, a friend who reflects the friendship of God in the lives of those around us. We'll discover what the culture gets wrong (and right!) about sisterhood, and I'll work alongside you to reject the temptations to compare and compete with other women. You'll also encounter stories along the way from women who share their personal experiences of friendship. These real talks — on everything from hospitality to friendship in times of transition — show the true diversity of authentic sisterhood.

It's not going to be as easy as spying a pair of matching shoes on the playground was all those years ago. But the gift of friendship is worth it. So, pour yourself a cup of coffee or two, and let's unwrap the gift of feminine friendship together.

Real Talk *with* **Krizia Rocha**

Healing in Friendship

I was hiding in my dorm on a Wednesday night from the college life that my Mexican-American, first-generation college student self was still completely perplexed and intimidated by. The walls kept me safe from the deep loneliness that was overcoming me during this huge life transition. Everywhere I turned, it felt like I had no one who truly understood everything I was experiencing.

That evening, my Facebook chat box opened up, showing a message from Amanda. We exchanged a series of hellos and she asked if she could come visit me on my college campus in Los Angeles. I said yes, of course. When she finally arrived, my insides felt somewhere between a first date and imposter syndrome. I was excited over the novelty of the friendship, but she also affirmed me so much and constantly commented on my beauty. Amanda had chosen me. "That's what I do for people," I thought, "but nobody has done it for me until now." Her visit was the beginning of a ten-year friendship and sisterhood.

When I first met Amanda, I didn't know the Lord. Much of our friendship was rooted in our large emotional capacity to receive the other and our bond over how much we loved to love (although we didn't yet know the fullness of what love was at the time). I hadn't encountered a friend who could match my emotional intelligence until Amanda. We stuck by each other through graduations, death and loss, first jobs, family hardships, breakups (primarily mine), and all the things life brings. Right after college, she married, and I was one of her bridesmaids. My reversion came shortly after her wedding and God took me by storm. Less than a year into my faith walk, I quit my full-time job and began to work for a pro-life crisis pregnancy center.

Amanda and I still kept in touch, but she and I were growing in different directions. Our intimacy became much more superficial. The yearning for a deeper and Christ-centered friendship was left as a yearning. It was so frustrating for my heart. All I knew at the time was how to stay because I had always felt unchosen and abandoned by friends. My fidelity was what I knew how to give her. I left Phoenix to start a missionary year and left her in God's hands.

We reconnected after my first mission year and I expressed my hurt in our friendship. She proposed we go to a praise and worship event in Orange County. As I drove, I could hear a resolute heart, a heart clearer in her need to take time to heal and be single with Jesus. Could this be the beginning of a new season for us too? But the events that followed that evening left me feeling helpless and lost in our friendship. A series of events thereafter led me to a painful conclusion. Amanda and I were transitioning away from our friendship that had been a constant for such a long season in our lives. I began to see I could not stay in a friendship that did not challenge me to grow toward heaven. I live with the hope that Amanda and I will someday reconcile, but I continue to focus on becoming the woman God made me to be, and the woman that I'm becoming. The more I become confident in who I am as his daughter, the more I grow in a desire for authenticity in my friendships.

There was much I learned about myself in this season with Amanda. But I also knew God was calling me to trust in his goodness when it came to friendships with women in my life. With time and healing, I learned that I believed friendship could not get better than Amanda, and that I lacked trust in the goodness of God. With time and healing, I grew in freedom, allowed myself to grieve, and sought closure from God and through my relationship with him. Freedom came as I took steps to move forward.

The season of friendship with Amanda that I was blessed with formed me for the rest of my life, and that is truly a gift!

Krizia Rocha, or Kiki, as most know her, is a Catholic woman on a mission to rebuild culture. She is an overcomer, and it is through her story of resiliency that she has found her calling to coach women into wholeness by cultivating their self-worth, mindset and dreams! Speaking is another one of her many loves. Having been brought up in a single parent home, being an abortion survivor and a sexual abuse survivor, she has much to share on how the modern-day woman is created for more. Bring her some babies and guacamole and you will make her happy!

1

Healing Your Heart for Feminine Friendship

We share our joys, challenges, thoughts, feelings, and crosses with the women in our lives. But even the healthiest and most authentic friendships can be frustratingly intricate, prone to miscommunication and misunderstanding.

Perhaps you cracked open this book excited to learn about the beauty of sisterhood. You may be facing friendship challenges, navigating difficult discussions with roommates, or experiencing hard seasons of transition with your friends after a big life event. Maybe you have a desire to grow deeper in relationship with the women you love as friends, taking your conversation past the surface level and truly encountering their hearts. Or you could be lonely, battling isolation, and looking for some practical steps when it comes to the nitty-gritty of friend-making as an adult.

You might be in the middle of discerning whether a friendship is healthy or not, searching for the words to say to transition away from a friendship while still honoring the dignity and story of a woman you're needing to take a step back from. Or, maybe you're wrestling with feelings of inadequacy after getting out of your comfort zone and making that vulnerable ask to be someone's friend, only to be rejected.

Whether you're in a steady place with friendship or you're not confident at all, each and every one of us always has room to grow when it comes to the art and genius of giving and receiving the gift of sisterhood. However, we're not going to start this conversation together by looking at our current friendships, exploring the practicals of healthy vulnerability, or navigating the muddy waters of a friendship breakup. At least, not yet. Don't worry, we'll get into all of those topics (and more!) in the upcoming chapters together. But first, we have to start by looking at our own hearts.

Yes, as counterintuitive as it sounds, the place to begin our conversation about sisterhood is to look at our own hearts and examine our own stories. We'll have conversations about defining friendship and even look at examples of women who speak about their own experiences. Before we can do that, however, we have to understand what it means to make a gift of ourselves.

"The person is unique and unrepeatable, someone chosen by eternal Love. The affirmation of the person is nothing but acceptance of the gift, which, by means of reciprocity, creates the communion of persons," Pope St. John Paul II explained during a general audience on January 16, 1980.[1] He sheds light on the beauty of reciprocal exchange and acceptance of the gift of the other, an exchange that we experience in healthy and authentic friendships with other women. But our ability to give and receive this gift of friendship is dependent on our ability to freely give and receive from a place of healed and holy wholeness.

If your story contains unhealed wounds from past friendships gone wrong, you won't be able to enter into a place of free, authentic, joyful, and trusting receptivity with another woman, no matter how many definitions you know or how many examples you read.

Does it seem selfish to start your journey toward loving others well by focusing on your own healing? The truth is, discovering these wounds not only can be instrumental in repairing your relationship with yourself, but can also impact your ability to understand and relate to friends from a place of wholeness and integration. With healing, you will be able to receive the imperfect, beautiful, messy gift of others and give your own very human heart in return.

Being able to interact with women from a place of healing instead of woundedness doesn't mean that our friendships in the future with women will be perfect or free from disappointment. The women you'll talk with, share your life with, drink coffee with, and go on walks with are human — which means friendship will inevitably include moments or tendencies toward frustration, envy, competition, or anger, among all the other emotions that we experience in our day-to-day life. That doesn't mean that those friendships are broken, it just means they're human. But when you're able to encounter those frustrating situations and emotions from a place of healing and not interact with them from a place of woundedness, your friendships with women will be able to not only survive, but thrive.

Maribel Rodriguez Laguna is a Licensed Professional Counselor Supervisor in Irving, Texas, where she is the co-owner of In His Image Counseling Center, PLLC. When I sat down to ask her about friendship in light of a Catholic understanding of counseling and therapy, she spoke into the danger of not being truly authentic in friendship, or holding part of yourself back out of fear.

"The gift of friendship is contingent upon a woman's ability to give of her true self," Maribel explained. "However, how can you give yourself authentically if the idea of who you truly are is tainted by psychological wounds?" If you've been wounded by women in the past, a natural response is to be guarded and hesitate from vulnerability to protect yourself. Or, you might hide from those parts of your story, pretending they didn't happen or don't affect who you are today. But avoiding painful parts of your past impacts your ability to see who you truly are as a beloved daughter of God. Giving the gift of your true self means giving a gift of your whole self — joys and sorrows, triumphs and crosses.

When you stay at a superficial level because of those wounds, you may avoid vulnerability and intimacy in friendship, which can lead to becoming overly independent. Conversations with other women could stay at a superficial level because of a fear of going deeper. You may wonder if someone would really want to be your friend if they really knew everything about you. When you live out of this woundedness in your relationships with other women, you can also struggle with perfectionism, fear vulnerability, and talk about yourself and others critically. "The journey of healing dispels the lies and helps a woman grow in strength, vulnerability with herself, and as a natural consequence, vulnerability with others. This deepens a woman's ability to give and receive love in friendship," Maribel explained.

Healing your heart for friendship means rejecting the lies and discovering who you truly are. Then you'll become stronger in your ability to be vulnerable with yourself, and in turn, vulnerable with other women. "You cannot give a gift of yourself first if you don't have an understanding of yourself. This requires a look into your personal story and an invitation into a journey of healing," Maribel explained.

Our healing journey begins by tracing the path of wounds throughout our story and inviting Christ, the Divine Healer, into our hearts.

Each one of us has a unique story as a Catholic woman, a specific path that has led us to where we are today. Many of us have been blessed with incredible examples of women in our relationships with our mothers, sisters, family members, friends, classmates, roommates, and neighbors. But those same relationships with women can also be relationships full of tension, pain, misunderstanding, and hurt.

Healing from Mother Wounds

More than likely, our mothers were the first women that we interacted with in our lives. Much of what we learn about relationship with women comes from our relationship with our moms. But your experience with your mother may include tense moments, misunderstandings, or even abuse. "Toxic mother-daughter relationships can come from issues with absenteeism or enmeshment," Maribel explained. "To use non-psychological terms, this would be when a relationship with a mother and a daughter included emotional abandonment or too much closeness."

These mother wounds not only impact the way that you view the women in your life, they also impact the way you view yourself as a woman. You may find traces of a mother wound if you struggle with a desire for acceptance and approval from the women in your life, after not receiving affirmation from your own mother. If you didn't feel loved by your mother, or felt less loved than your other siblings or family members, you might question whether your friends truly care for you.

Mother wounds can manifest in other ways, too. These wounds could include tendencies towards perfectionism as an attempt to gain acceptance, especially if you were only able to connect with your mother when you felt like you had earned her attention. If your relationship with your mom was particularly fraught, you could worry that even a slight misstep or unintentional mistake could ruin a friendship.

If you don't feel emotionally or physically safe around your mother, you might struggle with vulnerability in your friendships, feeling like you're on your guard and need to protect yourself. This can mean that you put your friendships through extensive tests to see if they are trustworthy. And, since your guard is up, you might miss or misunderstand another woman's attempts at openness and connection.

All of these ways that mother wounds affect us can seem overwhelming, especially since your relationship with your mom is so foundational to your other relationships and friendships with women. But even these deep wounds that trace back to the very beginning of your memory can be healed. If you find yourself wanting to dive deeper into this area of your story, I'd recommend picking up a copy of *Forgiving Mother: A Marian Novena of Healing and Peace*, by Marge Fenelon.

"A part of you was left behind very early in your life: the part that never felt completely received. It is full of fears. Meanwhile, you grew up with many survival skills. But you want yourself to be one. Whole. Integrated," writes Henri Nouwen in *The Inner Voice of Love*. As you examine your own heart and your own story, remember that you're worthy of a healing that honors your dignity as a woman and as a daughter of God. It's hard work. And it's a journey that may need to involve the help of a trusted mental health professional — at least it has in my own life. There is no shame in asking for help especially to sort through early memories and identify mother wounds.

Finally, if you have mother wounds in your story, you can find an incredible source of consolation in Our Lady. Your relationship with your mother may be a huge source of pain in your life — and even the best mothers make mistakes. But in the Blessed Mother we can find what whole, holy, and healed motherhood looks like. Free of sin, she is able to love each and every one of us as her child without a single selfish or ulterior motive.

It might take a while to turn to Our Lady, especially if you're experiencing deep mother wounds and find it difficult to trust any mother. Start with a small prayer that St. Teresa of Calcutta recommended: "If you ever feel distressed during your day — call upon our

Lady — just say this simple prayer: 'Mary, Mother of Jesus, please be a mother to me now.' I must admit, this prayer has never failed me."

Healing from Sister Wounds

While thoughts of sisterhood can sometimes send us into flashbacks of *Sisterhood of the Traveling Pants* and beloved literary characters like the March sisters in *Little Women*, it can also bring up not-so-perfect moments. In my family, I'm the oldest of six girls. There were (and are!) many light and joyful experiences of sisterhood like shared closets and late-night conversations about life over cups of coffee. But hard conversations, hurt feelings, and wounded hearts are also a part of our sisterhood. This reality of both the joy and frustration of sisterhood isn't something unique to my sisters and I, though.

"Conversations with sisters can spark extremes of anger or extremes of love. Everything said between sisters carries meaning not only from what was just said but from all the conversations that came before and 'before' can span a lifetime. The layers of meaning combine profound connection with equally profound competition. Both the competition and the connection are complicated by inevitable comparison with someone whose life has been so similar to yours and yet so different and always in your view," explains Deborah Tannen in her book *You Were Always Mom's Favorite: Sisters in Conversation Throughout Their Lives*, which contains interviews with over a hundred women.

Reflecting on your experience in your family of origin and your relationship with your sisters can provide some explanation for the way you interact in your friendships with women today. For instance, your parents or other adults in your life might have compared you and your sister frequently, asking why you didn't do something like your sister did, or advising you to make the opposite choice your sister made. If you felt like you weren't able to have your own experiences without being compared to someone else, you could see friends today as competition. Or perhaps your sister always worked through her frustration or disappointment with you because you were the closest available woman, even if you weren't emotionally mature enough to help her process those experiences. This might mean that you are hesitant to work through conflict or be present in harder conversations with friends today because you worry you won't have answers or know what to say.

Your sister might have handled problems with angry outbursts that you felt the brunt of, leading you to believe that conflict in your friendships with women can only be solved through loud arguments, insults, and firing off angry, emotional responses. As you grew up, you might have experienced feelings of rejection because your sister took a different path in life than your own. Or you may feel distant from a sister who married and moved away, or entered into religious community, shifting the way you communicate and relate to each other. In these seasons of change, you may wonder if you're worthy of friendship or somehow despised because of these changes in your relationship. This could lead you to hold fiercely, even possessively, onto your friendships with other women, afraid of them leaving or things changing between you.

Healing sister wounds in your story could mean including women in your healing. In addition to a therapist or counselor that you trust, you can build an intentional sisterhood of women who will accompany you as you heal. This accompaniment can be a reminder that healthy and holy friendship with women is possible, even if you've experienced wounds from your sisters. In other words, growing in these healthy relationships with women in your life can be beautifully redemptive.

"Healing will require that you build a support system outside of the therapy room," Maribel Laguna advised. "Start small and start now. Look for one supportive coworker, one supportive parish member, one supportive mom peer and one supportive friend. This compact support system will give you the foundation for authentic friendship and therapeutic success." The beauty of Christ's deep and integral healing when it comes to our wounds is that relationships with women can be transformed from a point of pain and rejection into a place of redeemed healing.

Healing from Friendship Wounds

Finally, some wounds that may need healing could have come from your friends themselves. Being hurt by those you trust is an especially deep wound because of the way that we as women rely on each other when things get stressful. In 2000, a group of researchers at UCLA discovered that when women face stressful situations, they respond by "tending and befriending" instead of switching into "fight or flight" mode.[2] This means that in moments of stress, women make sure those around them are okay and tend to their needs. But women also surround themselves with other women and build communities. Tending to and befriending other women in crisis situations also produces oxytocin, a chemical that boosts trust and empathy in our relationships. This natural feminine tendency to tending and befriending makes wounds from women you called friends all the more damaging. You may have expected to be received during challenging times or moments of vulnerability, but instead were mistreated, sidelined, or manipulated.

Maybe you opened up to a friend about a challenging situation you were going through, only to be ignored. If that moment of vulnerability was met with silence or a lack of empathy, you may be hesitant or even fearful to share what you're going through with other women. Similarly, you might have shared with a friend that you were wrestling with a sin, looking for encouragement and sisterly advice. But if you were met with judgment and made to feel less-than because of your struggle, it might be tempting to not open up and ask for help in your journey to holiness.

Or perhaps you trusted a friend and confided in her. If you later found out that your friend spread around what you confided to others, you may struggle to trust women, recalling the last time that your secrets were laid bare.

Maybe you were part of a friend group that grew and evolved as you got older, and you found yourself the odd one out, abandoned from a community that you once held dear. If you felt sidelined in that group of women, or were made to feel like your presence there was unnecessary or even unwanted, you may believe the lie that abandonment is unavoidable in friendship. This could lead you to avoid getting too close with women so that when conflict arises, your heart won't be as hurt.

If your friend or a group of friends in your life communicated in a way that was passive-aggressive, you may be confused in communication with other women in your life, too. It may seem like you always are second guessing, since you feel the need to read between the lines of every conversation, looking for a slight hint that things are going wrong, even if no one will tell you explicitly.

When you discover these wounds from your friendships with other women, you can invite Christ into those parts of your story and ask him to bring healing into your life. And as with mother wounds or sister wounds, navigating friendship wounds can also include the accompaniment of a mental health professional.

Authentic, trustworthy sisterhood is possible. As you find healing for these friendship wounds, you don't have to forget the way you were hurt by others, and the relationships you had (or still have!) with the women who hurt you may not magically change for the better. But as you discover those wounds and strive for healing, *you* begin to change. Healing from friendship wounds can help you grow in confidence and remind you that you're worthy of friends who truly tend to and befriend you in your challenges and rejoice alongside you in your joys.

Transforming Your Wounds into Worship
If you've identified places in your heart that have been wounded,

don't despair. These aren't destined to be forever challenging. It's actually these parts of your heart that the Lord desires to heal and radically transform. And even though the wounds might have originated from an experience of pain, the experiences that seem like immovable walls keeping you from receiving and giving authentic friendship are the exact places that the Lord desires to be invited into.

"Though the soul be healed, his wounds are seen afore God, — not as wounds but as worships," St. Julian of Norwich wrote in her book, *Revelations of Divine Love*. This radical level of healing and transformation of wounds to worship is something Christ's own story reveals as an incredible possibility, which can prove a consolation if you're sorting through your own heart and wounds in this chapter.

During his time on earth, Christ was abandoned by those he called his close friends. The people he chose to surround himself with for three years were the very people who betrayed him, abandoned him, and went back on their promises that they'd made him. When Jesus breathed his last on the cross, only one of his apostles remained. Since Christ was so aware of who he truly was and divine in his ability to give and receive friendship, this abandonment by those closest to his heart must have been excruciating. Paired with the heavy weight of the cross and the physical torture he endured, it's no wonder his Sacred Heart bleeds.

After his death, Christ rises from the dead and three days later, returns to the very friends who caused his heart such pain. Yet when he encounters them, he doesn't berate them for their poor friendship decisions or shame them for their choices. Instead, he stands in their midst and wishes them peace — and they're understandably startled and terrified. They think they're seeing a ghost come to haunt them.

But Christ asks them, "Why are you troubled, and why do questionings rise in your hearts?" And then he shows us what transformed wounds look like as worship, saying, "See my hands and my feet, that it is I myself; handle me and see; for a spirit has not flesh and bones as you see that I have" (Lk 24:38-39). The wounds on Christ's hands, feet, and side are not only the way that his disciples are able to recognize him; they also see how their lack of courage and loyalty impacted the very body of Christ. But with the grace of God, the vulnerability of Christ, and the transformative power of friendship and love, the apostles become overwhelmed with joy. They're able to heal from their own wounds of fear.

Christ desires to transform *your* wounds into worship, too. "Each one of us can experience wounds … that make us close ourselves off from God and others," Pope Francis said during an Angelus reflection in 2021. "Sin closes us in on ourselves because of shame, because of humiliation, but God wants to open our heart." Christ knows what it is like to be wounded by those he loves. Experiencing his tenderness and compassion opens our hearts to his work as the Divine Physician. There are no wounds too deep for the Lord to redeem.

Examining Your Heart for Friendship

Maybe you've experienced heartache from the women in your life who haven't honored your dignity as a daughter of God. But it's also important to remember that each and every one of us is wrestling with the reality of sin ourselves. Perhaps you, too, haven't lived up to the expectations of a good, authentic, and holy friend. How can you discover your own wounds and the ways you have wounded other women in your life by not reflecting the love of the Father?

If this conversation about wounds has left you hungry for a practical next step, examining your heart for friendship is a helpful place to start. While reading through this examination of conscience, you could note any places where your actions in friendship crossed the line into sin. Then, you can take these to the Sacrament of Confession. Although it's important to remember that if you didn't intentionally fail to mention a sin you were aware of in past confessions, you still made a good confession. Your sins were absolved by Christ through his priest, and God has forgiven you.

"When Christ's faithful strive to confess all the sins that they can remember, they undoubtedly place all of them before the divine mercy for pardon," the *Catechism of the Catholic Church* teaches in paragraph 1456. If glancing ahead at a long list of questions makes you nervous, don't despair! Another option is to read through this examination little by little, and when you encounter an idea that could help improve your friendship in the future, make a note and take the next right step.

For the times when my pride has damaged my friendships ... Lord, forgive me

- Have I believed the lie that I don't need friendship with other women, that I can do everything on my own without help?
- Do I believe that I'm the better woman in a friendship, superior to the other woman?
- Have I been slow to admit the ways I need to grow in the genius of feminine friendship?
- In moments of sororal correction, have I lorded my knowledge over a friend instead of encountering them with compassion, mercy, and humility?
- Have I diminished the gift of friendship someone gave me, while overemphasizing my sacrifices in the friendship?

For the times when my vanity and self-interest has harmed my friendships ... Lord, forgive me.

- Have I spent an excessive amount of time focused on my looks, comparing my body, story, gifts, and talents to those of women around me?

- Has the fear of what others will think of me motivated my words and actions in my friendships?
- Have I elaborated upon a story when talking with a friend so that I seem better than I am?
- Have I wasted time and resources in an attempt to keep up with trends, chasing what's popular in the present moment?

For the times when I have been envious of women in my life ... Lord, forgive me.
- Have I taken delight in hearing bad news about a friend?
- Do I suffer from morbid curiosity, anxiously scanning social media or conversations with friends for news of someone's misfortune or troubles?
- Have I failed to defend a friend in conversation when someone gossips about her?
- Have I envied another woman's gifts and talents, while being ungrateful for the gifts and talents that the Lord has blessed me with?
- Have I gossiped about another woman, willing others in the conversation to think less of her?
- Have I failed to keep the secret of a friend after she told me something in confidence?

For the times when anger has harmed my relationships with women ... Lord, forgive me.
- Have I lashed out at a friend, speaking angrily or hurtfully to them?
- Is there a woman in my life who I refuse to pray for?
- Have I ever tried to manipulate or control a friend?
- Have I felt hatred toward a friend, deliberately wishing bad things would happen to her?

- Have I intentionally stirred up conflict with friends?
- Have I interpreted the thoughts, words, and actions of my friends in a charitable way? Or do I assume the worst intentions of someone without considering the situation with compassion?
- Do I hold onto ways that other women have hurt me, resenting them and being unwilling to forgive them, especially if they've asked for my forgiveness?
- Have I let angry conversations fester in my imagination, reliving them after they have finished, getting angrier each time I revisit the words that were said?

For the times when apathy and laziness have infected my friendships ... Lord, forgive me.

- Have I tuned out during a conversation, letting my mind wander to other places when a friend is sharing something with me?
- Have I prayed for the women in my life and the crosses that they're carrying?
- Have I created an idol out of friendship, placing my friendship with women above my relationship with God?
- Have I trusted that the Lord will provide friendships in my life?
- Have I been inattentive to the needs of women in my life, thinking only of myself?
- Have I focused conversations on myself and my accomplishments instead of asking about the joys and challenges in my friends' lives?

For the times when I have been greedy in my friendships ... Lord, forgive me.

- Have I asked too much of a friend or inconvenienced

her intentionally?

- Have I calculated my investment in a friendship out of the desire to not be generous?
- Have I been obsessed with my comfort and well-being, to the detriment of sacrificing for my friends?
- Have I given to a friend grudgingly, emphasizing the sacrifices I'm making for her?
- Have I used friends to further my own ends and desires?
- In seasons of transition, have I taken the women in my life for granted?

Asking Forgiveness from the Heart of Jesus and from His Body

Maybe a certain friendship or conversation came to mind while you were examining your story. As you start anew on the journey to both give and receive sisterhood, a good first step is asking forgiveness for the ways you perhaps came up short.

As Catholic women, we're blessed with the beauty of the Sacrament of Confession. In confession, we ask and receive forgiveness not only from the Lord, but we also reconcile with the Church and her members. "Those who approach the Sacrament of Penance obtain pardon from God's mercy for the offense committed against him, and are, at the same time, reconciled with the Church which they have wounded by their sins and which by charity, by example, and by prayer labors for their conversion," the *Catechism* reads.[3] Confession is a great next step to take if something in this examination brought up a mortal sin, a sin which concerns grave matter that you have full knowledge of and gave your full consent to. If examining your heart for friendship stirred up an awareness of venial sins, praying the Confiteor (I confess to Almighty God, and to you my brothers and sisters ...) during the Penitential Rite at the beginning of Mass not only absolves those venial sins, but also reconciles you with the body of Christ, which surrounds you in the church while you pray for forgiveness and enter into the Sacrifice of the Mass.

Reconciling with members of the body of Christ is something Jesus desires for you, just as he desired for those he healed during his time here on earth. "During his public life Jesus not only forgave sins, but also made plain the effect of this forgiveness: he reintegrated forgiven sinners into the community of the People of God from which sin had alienated or even excluded them. A remarkable sign of this is the fact that Jesus receives sinners at his table, a gesture that expresses in an astonishing way both God's forgiveness and the return to the bosom of the People of God," the *Catechism* continues.[4] Confessing mortal sins in the Sacrament of Confession and asking for forgiveness during the Confiteor prayer at the beginning of Mass are both ways to reconcile not only with the Lord, but also with friends who are part of the body of Christ. Part of this process of reconciliation could also include asking forgiveness from the specific women you've hurt. It's vulnerable and sometimes scary to admit places where you've been wrong. I know, I've been there. Since I'm still figuring this whole holiness thing out, I know I'll be there again. But the beauty and power of asking for and receiving forgiveness is something truly amazing.

Medical studies reveal that receiving and giving forgiveness can lower your risk of heart attack, improve cholesterol levels and sleep, and reduce pain, blood pressure, and levels of anxiety, depression, and stress.[5] But those studies don't take into account the impact of forgiveness on our spiritual health. "The body, and it alone, is capable of making visible what is invisible: the spiritual and the divine," Saint John Paul said in his Theology of the Body audiences. "It was created to transfer into the visible reality of the world the mystery hidden since time immemorial in God's love for man, and thus to be a sign of it."[6] If our bodies heal, grow, and are restored by forgiveness, imagine the beautiful reality of forgiveness in the life of our soul.

When we receive the grace of God in confession, we're entering into a deeper friendship with him. By admitting where we have specifically wounded his heart and receiving his unconditional forgiveness, we're also reminded of the type of friendship our own friendships here on earth should mirror. "The whole power of the sacrament of Penance consists in restoring us to God's grace and joining us with him in an intimate friendship," the *Catechism* concludes. With God's grace at work, we can hope for restoration of intimate friendship in our friendships here on earth, too. And when we start from a place of healing and restoration, we grow in our capacity for sisterhood.

Receiving the Gift of Healing

Receive the gift of forgiveness. This could mean taking mortal sins to confession, intentionally praying the words of the Confiteor the next time you're at Mass, or simply accepting that Christ forgives your sins and your mistakes don't change the fact that Christ loves you and calls you his beloved daughter.

Giving the Gift of Healing

While you were reading this chapter on finding healing in your own story, a specific friendship in which you've hurt someone might have come to mind. Take this friendship to prayer this week and ask Christ to show you how you can best apologize to the women you've hurt.

Friendships That Remind You of Christ

In January 2012, I went for a routine twelve-week ultrasound to check on my second child. My husband had accompanied me to the first ultrasound with this child a few weeks earlier. Everything had looked perfect. I'd just started to wear maternity pants. And as the first trimester came to an end, it seemed my nausea was waning.

My husband didn't come with me to this appointment, because he was on a thirteen-hour flight home to Brooklyn from Hong Kong. I didn't mind, and I looked forward to having pictures of our littlest one to share with my husband when he came home.

It was surreal to learn that our baby wasn't moving and his heart wasn't beating when I had the scan. I cried in the sense that tears fell from my eyes, but I wasn't sobbing. I was stunned. I had an odd sense of peace that ultimately, things would be okay, but I was also aware that things were going to get harder before they got easier.

I called my family as I walked back to our apartment. My parents drove in from New Jersey right away, largely because they knew I'd be otherwise alone with our toddler until my husband's flight landed. We didn't have smartphones then. Talking to him would have to wait until the taxi dropped him off at our door.

In the days following, we realized we needed to tell the large group of friends with whom we'd shared news of the pregnancy that we'd lost our baby. Wanting to get it over with in one fell swoop, I searched my sent folder for the mass email we'd sent a few weeks earlier, the one with a photo of our other son in a "Most Awesome Big Brother" t-shirt attached. I typed a short, but direct, note explaining what had happened, asked for prayers, and hit send.

A few minutes later, a friend, but not a super-close friend, called in response. She was heartbroken for us, but I spent most of the short call feeling like I was reassuring her that we would be fine rather than receiving comfort and compassion. I hung up the phone and decided I didn't need to answer if anyone else called. Unless, of course, it was Sarah.

As if she could read my mind from her home in Boston, Sarah called right on cue. I don't remember what she said, but I do remember the feeling that she knew exactly what I needed and she'd dropped whatever she'd been doing to be there for me.

A week or so later, she took it to the next level. Sarah traveled from Boston to Brooklyn by bus to spend the time she could — twenty-four hours — with me. Later she would tell me that she didn't know what to say, but she knew that she could give her time, so that's what she did. She was just there. She was where I needed her to be, and that made me feel that I was where I needed to be in my journey of grieving and healing. We talked, we watched my toddler play on the playground, and we didn't worry about anything else for a little while.

Years later, I visited Sarah in her new home, Chicago. We spent a weekend together, either at my home or hers, once or twice a year, and basically talked the entire time we were together. Because we phoned and texted somewhat regularly in between visits, I knew it was a tough time for her. Her work situation wasn't great, and there were some other things weighing on her.

We put that aside for the weekend to shop, watch movies, and eat homemade macaroni and cheese. We laughed and enjoyed each other's company for two-and-a-half days, and then prepared ourselves to return to what "normal" looked like for each of us.

For me, this meant flying back to the East Coast to my husband and children, driving to school, and tying karate belts for lessons. For Sarah, it meant continuing to navigate a normal she was trying to find her way out of. I didn't realize how hard a time it was for her until I was leaving and our hug turned to tears. (This is a rare event; we often joke about her stereotypical Midwestern lack of outward emotion.)

I held on a little tighter, and realized I'd unwittingly been for her what she'd been for me. I was showing up because I loved her and wanted to be with her, but that visit meant something different and more profound for her.

Since then, I've been more conscious of what a gift this particular friendship is and I've made more of an effort to give what I can to it, even as our lives travel different paths.

I've learned that friendship as an adult is about seeing the other for who she is, especially when she can't do that for herself. It's about celebrating that in good times and affirming it in tough times. It's about listening without prescribing a resolution. It's about being there as fully as you can, and humbly trusting that the gift of seeing and knowing is exactly what the other needs.

Lindsay Schlegel is a daughter of God who seeks to encourage, inspire, and lift others up to be all they were created to be. She is the author of Don't Forget to Say Thank You: And Other Parenting Lessons That Brought Me Closer to God *and the host of the podcast* Quote Me with Lindsay Schlegel. *She writes for* Verily, CatholicMom.com, Radiant, *and more, and edits for Little Lamb Books and Ever Eden. Lindsay lives with her family in New Jersey, where she enjoys knitting, running, and reading to her kids. She would love to connect on social media or at lindsayschlegel.com.*

2

The Original Gift, the Original Giver

D id you know that there are over nine hundred Catholic churches packed into the 496.2 square miles that make up the city of Rome?

Imagine yourself on pilgrimage in the streets of Rome — an experience I was blessed to have with my husband and our six-month-old daughter a few years ago. (Yes, we braved a four-teen-hour flight with a squirmy six-month-old. Yes, we probably were crazy. But we had an amazing time and only messed up our sleep schedule for the next three months or so. Totally worth it.)

With the scent of espresso and diesel filling your nose, you spy the door to a small church, jampacked between storefronts and cafes. Stepping in, let your eyes adjust to the darkness. Then, take a few steps further into the echoing space and stop to stare agape at the beauty that fills every inch of the walls, floors, and ceiling around you.

While some of the churches you pass might be familiar — like the grandiose baldachin of St. Peter's Basilica or the jaw-dropping mosaics of Santa Maria in Trastevere — a majority of the hundreds (and hundreds!) of churches in the Eternal City are easily overlooked. Pilgrims wander past them on the narrow cobblestone streets, looking for a place to rest their aching feet and sip an afternoon cappuccino. While pilgrims and tourists alike might be tempted to spend most of their time in the breath-taking expanses of churches like the papal basilicas of St. John Lateran, St. Mary Major, and St. Paul Outside the Walls, the nondescript church hidden in a row of buildings on a bustling street can teach us something about the friendships we should strive for in our lives as Catholic women.

Many of these smaller churches don't even have the lights on. Some of the side altars, which are homes to glorious artwork by the masters, ask that you donate a few euros to press a button and illuminate the mosaics, frescoes, or shrines that sit in the darkness. When you put a coin in, and the light reveals the intricacies and talent of artists from years gone by, fellow pilgrims are drawn to the side altar like moths to a flame. The hidden beauty, waiting silently to be discovered in the shadows, is such a contrast to the well-lit Vatican Museums, or the public displays of famous art by masters like Michelangelo or Leonardo da Vinci found throughout the city. Yet on my trip to Rome, those hidden paintings that I strained to see, trying to make out the details through the darkness and dust, are the paintings I recall most vividly years after the trip.

It's not just the churches themselves that are hidden either. Even some of the saints who find their final resting place in Rome are tucked into nooks and crannies throughout the city. Some of the most famous household names go unvisited in churches that people pass by every day. St. Frances of Rome, a woman who dedicated her life to serving the poorest of the poor in the streets of

Italy, is buried in a hidden crypt in the Piazza di Santa Francesca. And despite multiple (failed!) attempts to find the body of Saint Cecilia, who is such a popular confirmation patron for girls, I was never able to in the two weeks that I spent in the city.

What do these quiet churches and tucked away tombs have to teach us today about the beauty of feminine friendship on this pilgrimage to heaven? As I leaned back and tried to relax on a fourteen-hour flight back home after two weeks in Rome, the lesson that struck me was one of hidden humility. The bodies of these saints, who dedicated their entire lives to the Lord, now seem almost forgotten. Hours of work from countless artists rest in the dark, unnoticed and overshadowed by larger and more impressive basilicas.

But these quiet, hidden tombs and frescoes are silent evangelists of the quiet, humble life of the Lord. There is something even more beautiful than any paintings and churches, which pilgrims can also pass by unknowingly. Miraculously, the very person who inspired the lives of the saints is present in those forgotten churches, too. Christ, under the appearance of bread, is tucked away in the tabernacle, his presence made known only by a little smoldering sanctuary candle.

Yet this is the paradox of Christian life: that the God of the universe would humble himself so much. Hidden in a tiny host, he waits for his creation to pause, marvel, and become more like the God in whose image they are made. But in our hurried rush, we often don't stop to simply sit and gaze at the humility of God. It's rare that we pause to let his humility penetrate our very souls and radically change the way we interact in our relationship with him and with others.

It's easy to marvel at the grand expanses of St. Peter's Basilica. Believe me, I know. I spent hours there just staring with my mouth hanging open, and returned to the basilica four times in the span of just a few days. Out of the hundreds and hundreds of pictures that I took on that trip, there are only one or two of the interior of St. Peter's, because I was so wrapped up in experiencing each and every moment that I forgot I even had a camera in tow. But just like it's easy to pass over the smaller, hidden churches, it's also tempting to forget the importance of the simple, humble life of the Lord here on earth and the weight of the Eucharist in our lives as Christians and in our friendships with women.

This Eucharistic reality is the cornerstone to understanding our friendship with other women and our friendship with Christ. To be in a place where we can both receive and give sisterhood, we have to first strive for friendship that is, at the heart, Eucharistic.

What does it mean to have our friendships founded in Christ? What would Eucharistic friendship look like practically in our lives as Catholic women? To discover the answer, we have to look at the life of Christ himself.

Christ's very beginnings on this earth were those of hidden humility. As I write this, it's evening and our little Advent wreath is across the table from me. Every year, we spend an entire liturgical season remembering the beauty of Christ's humility, and asking him to inspire the same humility in our own lives. We recall that Christ came to rescue us from our sins, taking on our human appearance. He didn't arrive with trumpet fanfare, or enter into this world in a posh nursery fit for a king. Instead, shepherds visited him as he rested in a feeding trough in a cave meant to shelter animals from the cold.

"Advent is the season of secret, the secret growth of Christ, of Divine Love growing in silence," Caryll Houselander reflects in *The Reed of God.* "It is the season of humility, silence, and growth. For nine months, Christ grew in His Mother's body. By His own will she formed Him from herself, from the simplicity of her daily life. She had nothing to give Him but herself. He asked for nothing else."

Christ's first precious moments on this earth were spent in the quiet womb of Mary. Our Lady could have easily boasted at the incredible reality growing in her body. Out of all women, God chose her to bear his son. She was (and is!) the epitome of human perfection, untarnished with a single sin. Yet instead of giving into the temptation of pride and boasting at the honor she'd received, she humbly accepts the possibility of a quiet divorce from Saint Joseph. Even when Joseph takes Mary as his wife at the direction of the angel in a dream, many assumed that Mary was carrying the son of Joseph, a carpenter, not the very Messiah the entire Jewish people had spent centuries and generations praying for.

Then she made the grueling journey to Bethlehem to give birth in a lowly stable. She could have complained, demanding more than a donkey to ride on as she carried the creator of the universe in her womb. Yet she was silent, quiet, contemplative. Everything she did, from carrying the infant Jesus in her womb to birthing him in a stable, points us back to the grace and presence of the Father.

In total humility, she exists within the lines and phrases of Scripture. She's the Mother of God, but we know very little about her life during the hidden years. In fact, one of the last documented stories of her motherhood is the story of how she loses Christ in the temple. Mothers everywhere can cringe at the last mention of their motherhood within the gospels being a time where their child slipped away from them for not one, not two, but three long days.

The God that Mary points us to with every fiber of her being is a God of incredible humility. Born to a humble family, raised in the home of a simple carpenter, he goes on to a life of public ministry where he's mocked, shunned, and avoided. The leaders of his religious community condemn him and spend their days obsessing over how they can trip him up. And finally, they seem to win when he's nailed naked to a cross, completely exposed to the world in seemingly utter shame.

As if that wasn't enough, Christ returns as the glorious victor over death and spends his remaining time on earth forgiving those who have killed him and strengthening his friends who abandoned him. Despite knowing that after his return to heaven, every single one of them would tremble in their faith and try to hide in an upper room, he gives the apostles the power and ability to call down his presence into a piece of bread at the utterance of a few simple words breathed over a small host.

Christ, the creator of the universe, could have chosen to be made present in the breaking of a fifty-course meal that takes weeks to prepare. But instead, in utter humility, he comes to us hidden behind the veil of bread, a meal so simple that even the impoverished widow can create it with a handful of flour and the olive oil that clings to the bottom of a jar (see 1 Kgs 17:8–24).

Christ extends us the ultimate and original friendship through his presence in the Eucharist. But he doesn't stop there. This isn't just an invitation into friendship with him. Instead, it's a model for our friendship with others, with the women in our lives. Yes, even in those friendships where we're struggling to give and receive the gift of friendship. Christ desires to give us the grace to be Eucharistic friends.

There are two components to this Eucharistic friendship to keep in mind as we explore what emulating Christ in this way means in our friendships. First, it involves growing in humility ourselves and considering the needs of others in our lives. This is Christ's invitation to make ourselves small and loveable, just like he does every day in the Eucharistic host. The second piece of Eucharistic friendship is that Christ himself dwells within us, which means that we can reveal him to others through the gift of friendship. Every single one of us, no matter our vocation or state in life, is to become what C. S. Lewis calls a "little Christ" to the women around us in friendship. Christ wants to transform each one of us as his daughters, "turning you permanently into a different sort of thing; into a new little Christ, a being which, in its own small way, has the same kind of life as God; which shares

His power, joy, knowledge, and eternity," Lewis explains in his spiritual classic, *Mere Christianity*.[1] We can become little Christs in all of our relationships, but let's explore the beauty of becoming Jesus in the quiet and hidden moments of our friendships. Thanks to Instagram, we might be tempted to think that the defining moments of our lives and of our friendships are found on a photo grid; that the success of our friendships is measured by how many pictures we share from a girls' weekend or a Sunday brunch. There's nothing wrong with girls' weekends or Sunday brunches — pour me a mimosa and let's chat over a cinnamon roll. But more than likely, the defining moments of the authentic friendships we crave are found off-screen. They're in the quiet conversations, the little details, and those hidden interactions of Eucharistic friendship. Away from a camera, we encounter Christ and reveal Christ to others in times of need — in those vulnerable asks for help, and the generous responses from the true friends in our lives.

It's in those small, hidden moments where the women around us are able to see not only us, but Christ acting through us. When you remember the detail someone thinks everyone forgot, or pause to spend time with a friend when you notice she's not doing well, you become Christ's hands, feet, and eyes. You become a little Christ.

This Eucharistic friendship isn't just something we give; it's also a gift we receive. In those moments where we beg Christ to be present in our words and actions, we also are allowed a glimpse of Christ hidden in the eternal soul of the friend who stands before us. When we see the face of Christ through the eyes of our friends or experience his presence through their friendship, that's when we're truly able to receive the gift of Eucharistic friendship. Those moments remind us of the true heart of holy, authentic, and wholesome friendships — the heart of God.

And just like we often forget the humility of God, we might also forget that our friends have immortal souls and will exist for eternity. What a thing to be hidden in our ever-changing bodies — a glimpse of the eternal nestled into our everyday interactions over coffee or a phone call. "Friendship is one of the lights in our earthly existence and gives us a faint foretaste of the Kingdom of heaven where love will reign supreme," writes Alice von Hildebrand.[2] The friendship we're aiming for, the sisterhood we're going to be diving into throughout the remaining chapters, reminds us that something greater is still to be grasped: eternity with our ultimate friend, the original gift and giver, Christ himself. We're aiming for what von Hildebrand is referencing when she says that "friendship is a remnant of paradise."[3]

If we don't grow in humility, not only are we going to miss out on the beauty of friendships with women in our life — we're also going to miss out on friendship and relationship with Christ.

And lest we think that this is a step we can just skip over on our way to authentic sisterhood, Fr. Cajetan Mary da Bergamo has a good reminder: "In Paradise there are many saints who never gave alms on earth: their poverty justified them. There are many saints who never mortified their bodies by fasting, or wearing hair shirts: their bodily infirmities excused them. There are many saints too who were not virgins: their vocation was otherwise. But in Paradise there is no saint who was not humble."

All of this talk about humility and letting Christ live his life within us *sounds* great, but how can we strive for this in our daily lives? You might be squirming at this point. But that discomfort stems from a misunderstanding of what it means to be a humble friend. Humility doesn't mean flattening yourself against the floor, letting people walk all over you, or thinking yourself as worthless. Instead, it's about spending less time thinking about yourself, with an emphasis on thinking of the presence of Christ in the person in front of you more.

I don't know about you, but I tend to ask for that humility timidly. Part of me longs for the trumpet fanfare for myself. My prayers for the virtue of humility remind me of my prayers for the virtue of patience. Usually, the Lord is very generous in giving me opportunities to grow in the virtue of patience. Sometimes, these opportunities come hard and fast enough that I can regret praying for the growth. But God doesn't humiliate or shame us when we ask for his grace to grow in humility. Instead, he reminds us of who we are as his daughters, and who he is as a good father, and a good friend. When Christ enters into our lives, just like he entered into the life of the Holy Family those thousands of years ago, he brings joy along with him. We don't pray for humility and wait for God to humiliate us. Instead, we can confidently pray for this Eucharistic humility and open ourselves up to receive the grace of God's love. He's going to remind us of who we are and *whose* we are.

Let's Get Practical

My spiritual director introduced the Litany of Humility to me years ago, with a warning to only pray it once a week at first. Once I read through the prayer, sitting in the church pew after spiritual direction, I realized immediately why it came with some precautions. It's a spiritual kick in the pants.

But sometimes that's exactly what we need in our interior lives — a wakeup call to remind us of the magnanimous friendship Christ desires for us. At least I know that's what I need on a regular basis. You don't have to face the Litany of Humility alone; let's go through it together line by line and really let the words resonate in our hearts and souls in a spirit of humble prayer and reflection.

O Jesus, meek and humble of heart, hear me.

Lord, you are the ultimate model of meekness and humility. We worship you, a humble God who desires for us to grow into your image and likeness, an image of humility and gentleness. Our desires for good friendship don't fall on deaf ears. Help us grow in your meekness and humility, not only in our relationship with you, but with the women who are or will be our friends.

From the desire of being esteemed, deliver me, Jesus.

Jesus, it's easy for us to believe the lie straight from the mouth of the devil that the praise of others determines our value. Free me from this trap and help me remember that you look at me and call me beloved — and that is enough. Then, inspire me to remind the women in my life that they're your beloved daughters, too.

From the desire of being loved, deliver me, Jesus.

Christ, you desire for me to love you above all things, and to love you with my heart, soul, mind, and strength. The love that I desire in my friendships isn't something bad that I should reject, but a love that I should rightly order. Help me remember that you are God, and not to put even good things on your throne in my heart.

From the desire of being extolled, deliver me, Jesus.

Lord, growing in humility means being rooted in the reality that you are God and I am not. Free me from the desire to be elevated and put on a high pedestal for everyone to see me. Instead, help me to shape my life in a way that puts you at the highest place possible, so that when others see me, they see you working through me.

From the desire of being honored, deliver me, Jesus.

Jesus, it's so tempting to take the seat of honor at the table and forget the dignity and value of those around me. It's easy to strive to "win" arguments or convince people of my worth in their lives as their friend. But I don't need a place of distinction or triumph in my friendships, Lord. Help me instead reverence you and accept the gifts and offerings of others in gratitude and humility.

From the desire of being praised, deliver me, Jesus.

Lord, when I'm tempted to use the gifts you've given me for the purpose of hearing the compliments and admiration of others, remind me that without you I can do nothing. These talents and gifts I have are gifts from you. When others compliment me, help me to accept those compliments with humility, and to always give you praise for the good that you've done in my life. Give me the grace to exercise my memory to more readily recognize and thank you for the ways you've lovingly surprised me with your good gifts in my life.

From the desire of being preferred to others, deliver me, Jesus.

Jesus, when I think of the women in my life, I struggle with the temptation to compare and compete. When I contemplate the stories of the women around me, help me to see the ways you've blessed them. Silence the temptation to be jealous of their talents and gifts, and help me instead rejoice and celebrate with them in the light of your goodness and faithfulness.

From the desire of being consulted, deliver me, Jesus.

Lord, I'm not you. I'm me — and I don't know everything. But you do, Lord. You know the workings of my heart and the movements of my mind. So, when I'm feeling dejected for not being the one my friend asked for help, remind me to turn to you with my friend so that, together, we can find all we need in your heart.

From the desire of being approved, deliver me, Jesus.

Lord, you and you alone define my worth and value and identity. In moments when I'm tempted to seek a stamp of approval from another, remind me to first turn to you to remember who I am in you.

From the fear of being humiliated, deliver me, Jesus.

Jesus, help me to love you for who you are as my dearest friend, and not just for the gifts you give me. Even in moments that are challenging and stressful, and especially in situations where I'm reminded of mistakes I've made, help me to lean on you and grow in the virtue of humility in the silence of my own heart.

From the fear of being despised, deliver me, Jesus.

Lord, your dearest friends betrayed, abandoned, and rejected you. When I know the ache of rejection, be my consolation.

From the fear of suffering rebukes, deliver me, Jesus.

Jesus, let me be so confident in my identity in you that you become my anchor. When sharp words are tossed at me, be a rock of refuge for me so that my peace and identity in you is not shaken. And when a friend rebukes me justly, help me to be receptive and to accept these words with a generous spirit.

From the fear of being calumniated, deliver me, Jesus.

Lord you are the way, the truth, and the life, and your truth stands firm. In moments when lies are uttered about me, remind me that I'm not alone, and that your truth remains.

From the fear of being forgotten, deliver me, Jesus.

Jesus, the women in my life will sometimes forget important dates, details, memories, and moments that we've shared together. But Lord, you always remember. My name is written in your hand and you don't forget.

From the fear of being ridiculed, deliver me, Jesus.

Lord, total surrender to you is a process and a journey. Help me surrender even how I am perceived by others. In moments when I'm ridiculed, help me accept the situations I cannot change as a chance to suffer with you and for you, to console your Sacred Heart.

From the fear of being wronged, deliver me, Jesus.

Lord, you are goodness, justice, and mercy itself. Help me to trust that you are always watching out for me, and that you permit only things that will work to your glory. Help me rest in that truth when it seems like all is going against me. Deliver me from the temptation to fix or control the situation.

From the fear of being suspected, deliver me, Jesus.

Jesus, help me not rush into conversations to correct others and make sure they are seeing me in the most favorable light. Instead, bring me your peace and your joy and remind me that my security comes not from what others think of me, but from you and who you are as God.

That others may be loved more than I, Jesus, grant me the grace to desire it.

Jesus, I know you love me and that you do not ration out your love. Help me to mirror your unconditional, overflowing love in my friendships.

That others may be esteemed more than I, Jesus, grant me the grace to desire it.

Jesus, remind me that praise from this world is fleeting, but I'm reflected in your eyes. Even when I'm not being noticed, give me the grace and courage to support the women around me and celebrate them.

That, in the opinion of the world, others may increase and I may decrease, Jesus, grant me the grace to desire it.

Jesus, give me the grace to grow in the humility of St. John the Baptist, who found joy and peace in a life of humility before you. In today's world that values vice over virtue, remind me that my value does not rest in what today's culture thinks of me.

That others may be chosen and I set aside, Jesus, grant me the grace to desire it.

Jesus, St. Thérèse of Lisieux desired that you treat her like she "was a cheap little ball which He could fling on the ground or kick or pierce or leave neglected in a corner or even press to His Heart if it gave Him pleasure." In moments where I feel like I'm the one neglected in the corner, help me to trust that your care and love for me never diminishes.

That others may be praised and I unnoticed, Jesus, grant me the grace to desire it.

Lord, when I feel hidden in the shadows of others, remind me of the hidden years of your life. Remind me that, hidden from the world, passing years without a single description documented in Scripture, you found deep joy in the quiet moments with your Holy Family.

That others may be preferred to me in everything, Jesus, grant me the grace to desire it.

Jesus, give me the courage to pray this prayer, and the humility to realize that you see me and you don't pass me by.

That others may become holier than I, provided that I may become as holy as I should, Jesus, grant me the grace to desire it.

Lord, help me rest in the reality that you know exactly what I need. I don't need to pretend that I'm you, in control of all things. Instead, help me become the saint you are calling me to be instead of the saint that I aspire to be.

Praying the Litany of Humility (and growing in the virtue of humility!) is challenging. But humility reminds us about who we are and who God is — as well as the identities of the women around us, who are all beloved daughters of God. The more we grow in our ability to give and receive sisterhood, the more Eucharistic we become, and the more Eucharistic our friendships become.

In Greek, the word 'Eucharist' (ευχαριστία) means "thanksgiving." The friendship we receive from women who will our good, who desire our growth in holiness, becomes a reason we turn to the Father over and over in thanks. When we grow in humility and littleness, we make space to allow Christ to live his life through us. We're able to strive to love the women in our lives the way that Christ loves him. Then, with Christ present at the heart of those relationships, our friendships can be a source of blessing for the women in our lives.

"Our life is linked to the Eucharist," St. Teresa of Calcutta wrote.[4] During her time on earth, Mother Teresa spent countless hours in conversation with Christ in Eucharistic Adoration. She also encountered him through Mass, receiving him daily in the Eucharist. Inspired by her example, we can also encounter Christ by spending time in Eucharistic Adoration at a chapel or parish nearby. Mother Teresa also dedicated her life to service, catching glimpses of Christ's face reflected in the men and women she served in the streets of India. When we strive to prayerfully receive Christ in the Eucharist and spend time with him in adoration, we can grow familiar with what Christ looks like and sounds like in prayer. When we spend regular time with the Lord, we'll be even more equipped to recognize, receive, and love him in our friendships with the women in our lives.

Receiving the Gift of Eucharistic Friendship

Every one of our friendships with women on this earthly journey back to the Sacred Heart of Jesus should mirror the incredible love that Christ shows us in the Eucharist. Make time this week to simply sit with Jesus in Eucharistic adoration for a few minutes. Don't worry about what you'll say or how you'll fill the time. Just exist with him and marvel at his humility, how he waits for you to stop by and share a few moments with him.

Giving the Gift of Eucharistic Friendship

Is there a moment in your life when a friend truly showed what it meant to be a Eucharistic friend? Today, reach out to her and thank her for that moment specifically.

Real Talk *with* **Amanda Zurface**

Friendships That Are Authentic and Holy

I grew up in the 90s. *Mean Girls* didn't release until my junior year of high school. I never saw it, but I certainly experienced unkind girls. I didn't give it much thought, though — I had my close female friends, and I tried to be nice to everyone at school. I know this is a gift, but I knew female friendships to be more like those in the *Sisterhood of the Travelling Pants*, *Fried Green Tomatoes*, and *The First Wives Club*!

High school ended, undergrad and graduate school came; friendships were natural and always available. I had close women in my life who told me that as they got older, friendships got harder. I didn't understand. I thought it was maybe due to a personality flaw or a personal problem. But graduation came and went, I accepted my first job, and adult life hit. Where were my friends? Most of mine were scattered throughout the world because of the schools I attended and my international interests. I was lonely and needed to step out of my introverted bubble, open my heart, and make a gift of myself in this new season of life. That scared me.

I immediately thought to pursue my friendships from middle school and high school, though those relationships had changed a long time ago.

An unspoken fear, and sometimes reality, is that our closest female friends are close and cherished until women find a better companion, specifically the one they wanted all along: their boyfriend or spouse. While friendships aren't always lifelong, and are often gifted to us in particular seasons, our female friends should not be disposable, taken for granted, or pushed aside when our helpmate comes along. We need each other.

Now, friendships change; there's no doubt about that, but I would argue we need to make the effort for ourselves and our friends, some who are taking active steps in discerning their vocation, or have married or joined religious life — all who may need you more than ever at this time in their lives.

I recently listened to a psychologist emphasize that friendships, with or outside your spouse, are the most important relationships to cultivate. Even with your spouse, the relationship begins as a friendship. And while we hope romance will always be there, it will most likely grow and morph into a beautiful and lifelong exclusive friendship, ultimately a more profound relationship than the fleeting romance. How do we learn to be the kind of friend our spouses and communities need? Other friendships teach us.

However, C. S. Lewis tells us in *The Four Loves* that few value friendships because so few of us have the opportunity to experience it.

Real relationships, like that of Saints Perpetua and Felicity, or idealized relationships, like that of Elsa and Anna in the Frozen movies, can be rare. But they are possible! You know how I know? I've experienced a friendship like this. In that season I mentioned, after college — when I needed to open my heart — I did, and God sent friends right in.

But months later, as I experienced a lot of hurt, betrayal, and confusion from an external situation, I pushed one of those very dear female friends away; she wasn't even a part of it. But I was hurting, and I didn't want to be vulnerable, transparent, or accountable. Even though this friend offered all of those gifts of a true friendship, and it could have been an instrument of healing I desperately needed at the time, I rejected the relationship, and ultimately her, because I was hurting so bad I couldn't accept her self-gift. I didn't have anything to give her in return, and that was scary.

When someone offers their friendship, don't take it lightly. She is making a gift of herself, and that is holy ground, because she's responding to God's invitation to love. Are you willing to give a gift of yourself in return?

Amanda Zurface, JCL, is the Catholic Content Specialist for Covenant Eyes. Amanda holds a License and MA in Canon Law and a BA in Catholic Theology and Social Justice. Amanda has served in various roles within the Catholic Church both in the United States and internationally. She is the coauthor of Equipped: Smart Catholic Parenting in a Sexualized Culture, Confident: Helping Parents Navigate Online Exposure *and* Transformed by Beauty. *She resides in Lexington, Ohio where she manages amandazurface.com: providing online spiritual direction and canon law consultation.*

3

What Makes a Good Friend Good?

I've been told to "find my tribe" by countless social media influencers, bloggers, and a Benedictine monk — no joke. But I don't want a girl tribe or a posse. I don't even have any #squadgoals. I honestly just want authentic friendship with women — something timeless, not a trend that I can slap a hashtag on. And I have a feeling you do, too.

Our desire for wholesome friendship is a good desire. And more than likely, when we think about the friendships that we want to foster and invest in, we aren't looking for drama, misunderstanding, miscommunication, and hardship. Although a good friend might be a challenge to define, it's easy to think of what we *don't* want included.

Much of what we think about friendships with women has been influenced by today's culture. Movies, TV series, books, and social media have all played a role in defining the ideal friendship.

It's easy to think of examples like Hilary and CC in *Beaches* or Mia and Lilly in *The Princess Diaries*. You may have grown up longing for adult friendships like what Monica, Phoebe, and Rachel had in *Friends*. Or, if you're a nerdy homeschooler or lover of literature like I am, you grew up wanting to find the Diana Barry to your Anne Shirley — a bosom friend and kindred spirit. If you were really lucky, you'd find a group of friends who channeled the energy and love of Louisa May Alcott's *Little Women* characters — a sensible Meg, creative Jo, virtuous Beth, and dear Amy, always trying to improve herself. That was the kind of sisterhood I longed for, probably inspired by far too many hours spent watching the 1994 film adaption and wishing I looked more like a brooding Winona Ryder while writing.

There are incredible examples of friendship between women throughout history, and even more unforgettable fictional examples. But what makes a friendship healthy? How can we define a good and holy friendship so that we know what to aim for? While there are countless resources for determining the health of a romantic relationship or family connection, there aren't as many resources for learning about healthy relationships with our friends, or discerning what friendships might need to end.

"While there are yards of books exploring the 'to end or not to end' question of romantic relationships, resources are scarce when it comes to friendship. This may be in part a consequence of the fact that friendships are often relegated to second-tier status in people's lives," explains Dr. Peg O'Connor, a professor of philosophy at Gustavus Adolphus College in St. Peter, Minnesota. "Romantic partners and families come first; friends get what is left over. The expression 'just a friend' cements the second-class status of friendships. Yet they do matter enormously."[1]

Just like any relationship, our friendships can range anywhere from holy and authentic to harmful and destructive. Our friendships with women matter. It's worth taking the time to not only examine our current friendships and see if they're sources of joy and holiness, but also to understand what makes a good friendship objectively good.

Determining the health, authenticity, and holiness of your friendships as an adult is a little more difficult than when you were younger. Back then, as long as you spent time playing together on the playground, you were set. Today, there are an incredible number of factors that go into discerning whether or not a friendship is leading you closer to Christ and helping you become the women that He's created you to be. However, there are some sure and certain things to look for when discerning the health of the friendships you have, and equipping yourself for future good friendships.

Since friendship is a gift that we both give *and* receive, it's important to keep in mind as you read through these qualities of a good friend that these are also characteristics to grow in yourself. If you're looking for a friendship founded in Christ, you have to find your foundation in Christ, too. Because sisterhood is a two-way street, you can't expect these qualities if you're not prepared to give in the same way yourself.

Authentic Friendships Are Rooted in Christ

Aristotle, a Greek philosopher who lived in the fourth century BC, believed that there are three types of friendship: friendships of utility, friendships of pleasure, and friendships of virtue.[2] Friendship of utility is based on the good that you receive from a friend, or an advantage from your relationship with her. This is the friendship you might experience with a coworker. You enjoy working with her and bond over shared projects, but if you were to quit your job, there's a good chance you wouldn't keep up with each other. Meanwhile, friendships of pleasure are centered around a good time experienced together. For instance, you might be friends with women who are in a group class together at your gym, or the woman reading at the coffee shop every week who you make small talk with as you wait for your latte. You share something in common that brings you pleasure — that is, if you find the gym pleasant! — but if you were to stop going to that gym, or switch up coffee shops, your friendship would more than likely dissipate. Friendships of utility or pleasure aren't bad, but they aren't permanent. What is helpful or useful to us evolves as we grow, and what is pleasant and enjoyable to us also changes.

Then, there's virtuous friendships. Even though Aristotle lived three hundred years before the birth of Christ, he recognized the beauty and value of friendship grounded in something outside of ourselves, something higher. "Perfect friendship is the friendship of men who are good, and alike in virtue," he explained. Friendships of virtue are not as fragile as friendships of utility or pleasure because goodness and virtue are things that endure. Objective goodness is good, regardless of what job we work or what we do for fun on the weekends.

While a desire for virtuous friendship can spring up in us quickly, the building and maturing of that friendship takes both time and familiarity. Aristotle reflects on a proverb that says you can't truly know your friends until you've "eaten salt together." He doesn't mean that you should crack open a bag of salt with the person that you're trying to become friends with and sit there and eat it all for instantaneous friendship. Instead, this proverb refers to the tiny amounts of salt we add to our meals, which shared over a lifetime, would result in a bag of shared salt. Through shared time together, we discover the women in our life who are lovable and trustworthy, who live through the good and bad together, and desire our true happiness and joy.

Throughout his writing, Aristotle reminds us that authentic friendship that lasts has to be rooted in virtue, and a desire for virtue that we share with our friends. For us today as Catholic women, this means that holy and wholesome friendships will always find their foundation in Christ and a shared vision of striving for holiness in our everyday lives. These are the friendships that are Eucharistic, like we talked about a few pages back. This doesn't mean that we can't be friends with women who aren't Catholic or even Christians. In fact, Christ commissions us in the Gospels to share the light and truth of faith with everyone we encounter, and that evangelization happens through encounters with others and growing in relationship with them. Friends who aren't Catholic can be an amazing source of encouragement, conversation, and accompaniment. They can show you different perspectives and through their curiosity about your faith give you opportunities to discover what the Catholic Church truly says about the big issues of life. But the deepest and most virtuous friendships we can have are with other Catholic women who share our desire for sainthood as the end goal.

What does this Eucharistic friendship look like practically? Let's take a look at Marie Guérin, St. Thérèse of Lisieux's cousin. Like Thérèse, Marie discerned a vocation to religious life and entered Carmel in 1895, taking the name Sister Marie of the Eucharist — which makes her an even more perfect example of Eucharistic friendship. She spent her novitiate under the guidance of Thérèse, who was responsible for training the younger women in the convent. Sister Marie's letters give us incredible insight into the suffering and death of Thérèse in 1897. Eight years after Thérèse's death, Sister Marie also died of tuberculosis.

During her time in the convent, Sister Marie of the Eucharist corresponded with a woman named Céline Pottier, Thérèse's childhood friend and Sister Marie's cousin. They exchanged many letters back and forth, and their correspondence reveals a true understanding of holy, authentic friendship.

Commenting on her friendship with Céline, Sister Marie wrote: "Oh, as you so well said, the friendship we have is no ordinary friendship; it's a friendship between souls. It was God who united our souls, and it is God who helps you to understand so many things that are incomprehensible to others, because, as I've said many times, He chose your soul. He loves you with a special love, and don't forget that He expects a great deal from you because He has given you a great deal. He wants us to help each other become saints, and that's why He made our souls in sympathy."

Have you been blessed with a friend who is the Céline to your Sister Marie, a true soul-level friend? Sister Marie puts the grace and gift of this kind of friendship into words so beautifully when she describes it as a result of God making her and Céline's souls "in sympathy." The word "sympathy" comes from the Greek language and describes the idea of having shared feelings within a community.[3] This means that joys, sorrows, crosses, and celebrations aren't something that you have to process alone — they're emotions and experiences you can share with true friends. This is Eucharistic friendship — healing balm in our lives, with the origins of that healing rooted in the sacrifice, mercy, and love of Christ who suffers for us and with us.

Her friendship with Sister Marie of Eucharist also influenced the way that Céline discerned friendship with women in her life. Céline was married to Gaston, an attorney, and together they had two daughters. In another letter between the two women, Céline wrote to ask about whether or not to befriend another lawyer's wife.

In response, Sister Marie wrote back, advising: "You asked me what my opinion was on the subject. Here it is: if this lady loves the world and is worldly, I would, in a word, advise you not to spend a lot of time with her. You would gain nothing from it, be led astray, and all the conversations would leave you with an empty heart and a head full of trivialities. ... But if this lady looks after her soul and her family, only takes from the world what her position requires, and above all, oh, above all, doesn't love the world, you can befriend her without fear."

Authentic friendships — the kind our hearts are hungry for —

find their foundation in Christ. Look for women who are striving to become the women Christ created them to be. If they're investing in their friendship and relationship with Christ and desiring holiness, then you can confidently enter deeper into friendship without being afraid.

And above all, remember that friendship with other women that is rooted in Christ and in virtue doesn't happen by chance or by our making it happen. "For a Christian, there are no chances," C. S. Lewis reminds us in his book, *The Four Loves*. "A secret master of ceremonies has been at work. Christ, who said to the disciples, 'You have not chosen me, but I have chosen you,' can truly say to every group of Christian friends, 'You have not chosen one another but I have chosen you for one another.' The friendship is not a reward for our discriminating and good taste in finding one another out. It is the instrument by which God reveals to each of us the beauties of others." The gift of virtuous friendship rooted in Christ is a gift from Christ himself. If you've been blessed with women who are virtuous friends, thank Christ for that gift. And if you're longing for that kind of friendship in your life, ask the Lord to send it to you.

Authentic Friendships Make You a Better Woman

Friendships that are rooted in Christ have the capacity to be transformative. When you're receiving and giving the gift of friendship with someone who is striving for holiness and authentic friendship, not only will you discover her feminine genius and gifts, you'll also discover and become the woman God has created *you* to be. But the journey of becoming that woman usually involves a little pruning, the weeding away of what is keeping you from the heart of Christ and from entering into friendship fully.

It could be that you're giving into vices, going back on promises you made to others or yourself, or speaking negatively about yourself. A good, authentic friend offers kind (but clear!) sororal correction when she witnesses you not living like the woman God created you to be.

St. Teresa of Ávila had some advice for these conversations for her sisters living in the community together. She wrote, "True friends correct each other when it is necessary. They realize that Gospel admonition is an act of love, nothing less." Healthy friendships are rooted in the love of Christ, which constantly wants the other's good. So, even if the conversations are awkward, good friends help you become not only better, but more authentically yourself.

A true friendship reflects the love of God — a love that calls us to be perfect as he himself is perfect. This means that there has to be some element of sororal correction in the event of conflict. And trust me, even among the best and most holy of friendships, there is conflict. If there's human beings involved, you'll eventually rub each other the wrong way. But a good friend doesn't let the pain fester. Instead, in total charity, she brings it up to you and explains her experience of your actions.

"Friends share the same interests; but more than that, they are so interested in the welfare of the friend that they truly share his joys and sorrows," von Hildebrand writes. If you're desiring wholesome and holy friendships, seek out friends who are interested in your joys, sorrows, and eternal soul.

Authentic Friendships Include a Shared Sense of Trust

Von Hildebrand valued trust in her relationships so much that she called it the key to perfection that characterizes both love and friendship. "Trust. This word is a gem and sheds light on the deepest human experiences. 'I believe' is an act of trust," she wrote. "No human relationship, be it love or friendship, can survive if the 'trust' that one had given to another person is sapped and ultimately destroyed."[4]

Oftentimes, this trust isn't built in huge emotional moments, but instead, in small acts of trust. Dr. John Gottman, who has spent more than thirty-five years studying healthy relationships, calls these small opportunities of trust-building "sliding door moments," referring to the 1998 movie *Sliding Doors* starring Gwyneth Paltrow. Her character in the film lives two alternative lives after missing a train one day. Dr. Gottman defines these moments as "seemingly inconsequential everyday incidents or decisions that affect relationships negatively or positively."[5] It's in these little moments that trust is built in our friendships with women.

Maybe your friend from college remembered to check in on how your mother is doing after a surgery, or a woman you're getting to know from a small group followed up to let you know that she prayed for you after you shared something challenging that you're processing. Those sliding door moments might seem small and insignificant, but collectively, they can reveal the levels of trust you share with the women in your life.

Trust is made in small moments of connection, and it's also a gift that is given and received in the context of friendship. So, as you discern the friendships in your life, remember to zoom in and take a look at the little moments of trust building when a friend honors your relationship by showing themselves worthy of trust.

Authentic Friends Listen to Your Story and Encounter Your Heart

Every single one of us will need help at some point or another. Maybe we're in need of a lift after a car breakdown, or someone to laugh over a joke we can't keep to ourselves. But often, what we really desire is someone to encounter our story and listen to what we have to say.

In healthy friendships, you feel an inner urge to share with the other. Women in authentic friendship receive the news of the other, whether that's big or small. You'll notice that the women you trust to share your story with are good listeners, they don't interrupt you, and they simply listen to listen. Instead of listening to solve the problem or form a response, they encounter your story and exist in the present moment with you.

In 2010, Charles G. Gross conducted a study and found that there is a time delay between what we hear and what we understand when someone shares something with us.[6] You might be a fantastic listener, and this time could be just a few seconds. But for others, it could take up to a minute to process all that someone has shared with you. When we listen just to formulate a response, we don't allow ourselves time to process what the other has said, or respond with charity and intentionality.

Look for (and pray for!) friends who are gifted with the ability to receive you and your story, who don't just listen for a pause in your sharing so that they can interject their thoughts or opinions. Instead, they receive you and encounter your story with the compassionate heart of Christ.

Authentic Friendships Champion Your Vocation

Often, friendships begin when you're sharing the same season of life. How many of us have friends that we met when we were in the same grade in school, or the same class in college? Or maybe you met your best friend when you both started at a new job together. But, as life goes on, sometimes seasons change at different times for different people. These seasons of transition can be challenging, but beautiful! Don't worry, we're going to take a deep dive into different seasons of transition in the next chapter. For now, it's good to remember that authentic friends encourage you in your vocation, regardless of whether you're in the trenches of the same season or striving for holiness at different places in the journey.

If you discern a call to religious life, authentic friends journey alongside you throughout the discernment, even if that means surrendering what your friendship looked like before you heard the

Lord calling you. When Christ asks you to be present in a season of singleness, authentic friends receive your story, rejoice in your joys, and help you carry your crosses. If the Lord is inviting you to discern the vocation of marriage, conversations with authentic friends are void of put-downs of your spouse. In authentic friendships, vocations, missions, and families are not a source of competition with your friend. Instead, these conversations and friendships are places of encouragement that inspire you to go home and love your spouse and your family even better than before.

Authentic Friends Support You as You Carry Crosses

French author Jean de Rotrou once wrote, *L'ami qui souffre seul fait une injure à l'autre,* "the friend who suffers alone insults the other." When we put up a false front of "having it all together," we rob our friendships of the ability to grow through shared suffering. Christ doesn't promise his followers an easy path. In fact, he explicitly shows us that we'll carry our own cross if we follow him. But he never says we'll carry these crosses alone. Even on his own journey to Calvary, Christ received the gift of friendship from Simon of Cyrene, who physically helped carry the wooden beam of the cross for him.

There is no hiding of suffering or the reality of the cross from authentic friendships. Because these friendships rejoice in a shared healthy trust and vulnerability, they are places where you can receive all of the other woman's story, including the challenges and crosses that she is carrying.

If you're looking for authentic friendship, keep an eye out for the women who suffer with grace. These are women who are intimately aware of the weight of the many crosses Christ asks us to pick up and carry on our way back to him. Not only can they offer solace in challenging moments on the journey, they also know how to come alongside you as your Simon of Cyrene.

Authentic Friendship Doesn't Calculate

In Scripture, Christ says that there is no greater love than laying down one's life for one's friend (see Jn 15:13). In order to strive for this ideal, we cannot carry a calculator around in our back pocket. Our sisterhood cannot involve keeping score of who is the better friend, who has sacrificed more, or who has done more for the other, if we're to live authentically as daughters of God.

"Not only is it against the genius of friendship to calculate, but moreover our fallen nature always tempts us to misread a situation to our advantage. 'I am the greater giver.' This attitude alone shows that the friendship is flawed," writes von Hildebrand.[7] The sacrifice that authentic sisterhood demands is never outdone in generosity, just like the Father's love for each and every one of us. Authentic friends give the gift of friendship to other women, not so they can receive exactly what they gave back in return, but so they can mirror the unending generosity of God in the lives of those they love.

"One of the great dangers in friendship is to exchange roles, as it were. The giver should downplay his sacrifice: 'I was happy to do so.' And the receiver should carefully refrain from minimizing or demeaning the gift received," von Hildebrand writes. "From this point of view, the desirable response of the giver should be the very opposite response of the beneficiary. Too often, people reverse these roles. Some givers like to magnify their efforts or their gifts, and the receiver can be tempted to play them down."[8]

This lack of calculation doesn't mean having a lack of boundaries, or letting someone step over and on top of you in the name of false humility. Instead, it means approaching friendship asking what you can give the other instead of worrying or focusing on what you will receive. Authentic friends strive to outdo each other in generosity and have the self-awareness to recognize the flaws in the gifts that they give, which allow space for Christ to make up for what is lacking.

Authentic Friendships Don't Fulfill or Satisfy You

Did that sentence catch you off guard? It's important to remember as we examine our friendships that we can't expect total and unconditional love from a human being. Even your best, most loyal, authentic friend isn't capable of that level of love. But that doesn't mean that your desire for total and unconditional love is bad — only that you have to seek its fulfillment in the right place. We can only find totally fulfilling friendship in the Sacred Heart of Jesus.

When we expect a friend to love us in a way that only God can, we're turning our friendship into an idol. We're placing that friendship and our expectations of it higher than our love of God and our trust in Him alone to satisfy us. Yes, our friendships are called to reflect this total love of the Father, but they can't be idols that stand in the way of our relationship with God. Instead, our friendships with the women in our lives are called to become icons — a relationship that draws us further up and further into friendship and relationship with our Creator.

Sisterhood is a gift, but it's not the ultimate gift. However, the best friendships — those that are Eucharistic and rooted in a friendship with Christ — are the ones that will reveal the love of the Father here on earth and remind us of the joy of eternal friendship in heaven.

Ordering Our Friendships Rightly

Now that we've taken a look at what makes up authentic friendship, it's also important to touch on the fact that it's natural (and normal!) for there to be a hierarchy among your friendships. That sentence might make you squirm, but von Hildebrand explains this hierarchy in a way that beautifully honors the gift of every single friendship.

"Those whose life has been blessed with many friendships realize that while all of them are gifts, there is nevertheless a huge hierarchy among them; all should be gratefully welcome, but one will inevitably perceive that whereas all flowers are loved by a gardener, there is a huge difference between a lily and a daisy," she writes. "This is not to deny that any tiny little ones should not be gratefully greeted, but the notion of hierarchy — so easily or even purposely ignored today in the name of 'democracy' — should never be forgotten in human existence. St. Teresa of Ávila in her great book, 'Interior Castle' tells us that in heaven no two persons will have the same degree of glory."[9]

As you read this book and encounter examples of authentic friendship within the stories of women or the writings of the saints, some current friendships may come to mind that aren't authentic and holy. In fact, some of the women in your life may not even be living up to the definition of a true friend. If you've realized that your friendships have room to grow or might even be entering into a season of pruning and change, what's next?

First, take time to examine exactly what in your current friendship is causing it to not be a friendship that is rooted in Christ or a relationship where there is a shared giving and receiving of true selves. Just like we opened the book with an examination of our own heart, a good place to look first is at our expectations of friendship. It could be that you're expecting too much of a person and demanding more from the relationship than she can give.

"We could say that each friendship symbolizes a certain number of talents: ranging from one to ten. It is crucial that this is perceived in our relationship with others, for there is a tendency in most of us to demand more than our friend has received and therefore can give," von Hildebrand explains. "It is made clear in the Gospel that when the Master comes back, and exacts accounts from his servants, he will not ask the one who has received only one talent to give him back two. But he will rightfully be very displeased if the one who has received ten give him back only nine. Maybe some friendships break up because one friend, failing to perceive the number of talents his friend has, demands more than what he can give. How unfair to expect the perfume of a lily from a daisy: and yet, the daisy should be appreciated and viewed as a gift of God."[10]

This isn't to say that you shouldn't desire holy and wholesome friendships with the women in your life. In fact, you should desire that for your friendships. But in a particular example of a friendship that is a challenge or in need of healing, first determine whether you are expecting too much from that relationship in its current season. We don't expect ourselves to climb the stairs if we're in a wheelchair, and we don't expect our favorite sports hero to play front and center if they're recovering from an injury. So too we have to make sure as we navigate friendships that are challenging that we have realistic expectations for ourselves and our friends.

There is a difference, though, between adjusting expectations in a friendship and discerning whether or not a friendship should be in your life. When you see all the ways that your friendships need to grow or the wounds that other women have inflicted on you, it's tempting to cut all ties and move on with the hopes of making better and authentic friendships with new women. But be slow to label someone in your life as "toxic," a word that's become popular in our vocabulary these days. Sure, it seems easy to just walk away from a friendship and cut that person off completely from your life. But what might be needed are some healthy boundaries and adjusted expectations.

Boundaries in friendships might seem like barriers to authentic relationships, but usually in friendships that we desire to grow, boundaries can in fact be incredibly helpful and connective. Dr. Brené Brown is an author, speaker, and researcher on the subject of shame. She defines boundaries as "What's okay and what's not okay." She explains that boundaries "are not fake walls, they're not separation, they're not division — they're respect." [11]

Setting boundaries in a friendship means you will need to have intentional conversations with friends in order to grow. It can be tempting to shrug off hurts or pretend like nothing happened. But being clear and kind with these women is giving the gift of friendship to them, and loving them in a way that encourages them to grow in holiness, to become more like God. If you pretend that something a friend has done that hurt you isn't a big deal, or brush it off with a dismissive "don't worry about it," you're not giving your friendship the chance to grow through both that honest conversation and the process of forgiving and reconciling. And since you're hiding the fact that you were offended or injured, you're not giving your whole self in the friendship. If you avoid those straightforward (and sometimes challenging!) conversations, you run the risk of injuries festering until you simply can't take it anymore and walk away from the friendship without any resolution or closure. Skirting around the topic of boundaries can do much more harm than help.

Most of us don't know how to establish a good boundary with a friend. It's natural for us to think about that conversation about boundaries from our friends' perspective. But if we let worry and concern about how the conversation will be perceived keep us from ever having the conversation, we're not being a good friend to that woman. We're not being honest with her, or giving her the chance to encounter our hearts or our story. Instead, we're practicing false humility and harming the friendship.

"We can't manipulate people into swallowing our boundaries by sugar coating them. Boundaries are a 'litmus test' for the quality of our relationships," Henry Cloud explains in his popular book, *Boundaries: When to Say Yes, How to Say No To Take Control of Your Life.* "Those people in our lives who can respect our boundaries will love our wills, our opinions, our separateness. Those who can't respect our boundaries are telling us that they don't love our nos. They only love our yeses, our compliance. 'I only like it when you do what I want.'"[12]

Striving for clear communication in our friendships with women can be difficult, especially if there is a wound you're still healing from. But with the help of prayer, discernment, and perhaps the advice of a trusted counselor, boundaries and hard conversations can transform a friendship. Instead of labeling the friendships in your life that aren't living up to their full capacity as "toxic" and walking away from them, first take the time to discern whether they can be healed with the help of communication that honors the dignity of the friendship, and boundaries that respect everyone involved.

Ending Friendships with Grace and Dignity

Friendships that are good to their core are worth fighting for. But relationships with women who don't treat you like a daughter of God and honor your dignity — even after clear communication and boundary setting — are friendships to transition away from.

Breaking up with a friend who isn't treating you well is challenging. In fact, the emotional load of breaking off a friendship with a woman who you used to consider a friend is similar (and sometimes greater!) in intensity to that of a romantic relationship breakup.[13] And while there are podcasts, blogs, and even country music songs to help you process a breakup with a boyfriend, resources for sorting through the practical details and emotional load of ending a friendship are few and far between.

If you've defined, established, and enforced boundaries with a friend, only to have her argue, reject, and dismiss those boundaries, it's time to take a step back. A woman who isn't interested in respecting the boundaries you establish for the good of your relationship is not in a place where she can fully give and receive the gift of friendship. Without this mutual desire for a healthy relationship, there cannot be a friendship. In fact, if a woman is giving you grief for your boundaries or selfishly manipulating them, the relationship between you two doesn't actually deserve the label of friendship anymore. Sometimes recognizing that truth can make taking a step back a little easier to navigate.

One way to take this step back is to quietly distance yourself from the relationship. If you're the friend who initiates get-togethers or conversations, you can allow your friendship to naturally fade if you stop initiating. When I spoke to women I know and trust during the writing of this book, they mentioned that this is often how their friendships end. However, this isn't the only way to take a step back. You can also have an honest conversation with your friend, which can provide some much-needed closure to the relationship.

Here is the part of the book where I wish I could give you a quick bullet point list of conversation topics to kick start that final conversation. Or you might wish that the next few paragraphs were text that you could copy and paste into a succinct goodbye message. But I can't give you the exact template for how to navigate this friendship breakup. If you're frustrated by that, I get it. I've been in your shoes, discerning the end to a friendship and combing through online resources looking for someone to just tell me what to say to make this easier. But the reason that I can't include that specific of a resource is because you are a unique woman, gifted with certain charisms and temperaments, asked to carry specific crosses and bear certain sufferings in your life. You come from a unique family of origin and have lived through unique friendships in your life. And so has the woman who you're struggling with.

I could share with you all of my favorite books, online articles, and podcasts on the subject of friendship (check out the footnotes as you read through each chapter and you'll find them!) but at the end of the day, your friendship is between you and your friend. There isn't a one-size-fits-all way to end a friendship because there's not a one-size-fits-all way to be a friend as a Catholic woman. Yes, there's the one-size-fits all universal call to holiness. But the reality of the unique way that plays out matters when you're discerning who you can give and receive the gift of friendship with.

However, despite my inability to provide you with the exact

words and template of a friendship breakup, there are some universal principles to keep in mind. The first is to pray. Pray before you take a natural step back and quietly let the friendship fade. Pray before you have that final conversation. My parish priest once shared that when he asked his spiritual director for advice on how to navigate a hard conversation with a friend, he was told spend 90 percent of the time praying for the person he was going to talk to, and only about 10 percent of the time actually talking to them. If you're sensing you need to end a friendship, pray. Bringing up hard topics and sorting through the emotions surrounding the end of a friendship is challenging, and it's something you can only do well if Christ is acting and living through you. So, make space for him in your heart and in your day by dedicating some serious prayer time for this woman and the end of your friendship with her.

Another thing to keep in mind that applies to all friendship breakups is good communication skills. Make sure to start your sentences with "I" instead of "you" to avoid accusatory statements. Remember to listen to her perspective if she shares something with you in your conversation together. Treat her in the way you want to be treated in this conversation. And although it sounds simple, remember to take deep breaths throughout the conversation and stay present in the moment, as much as you might want to run for the door or at least mentally escape from the situation.

You might be navigating an incredibly difficult friendship breakup and having that last conversation for closure isn't possible. If this is the case, you can still follow everything mentioned above. Pray for this woman and for her to experience peace and joy in her life. Then, using those same communication principles, sit down and journal what you wish you could have said to her. Or, you could write those words down in a letter form to her, even if you never send that letter to her to read.

Just like you need to be clear and kind with the establishment of boundaries in a friendship that can be salvaged, you can (and should!) also strive for clarity and compassion in the relationships that can no longer be labeled friendships. Labeling someone as "toxic" and walking away without a moment's notice can seem tempting, especially if conversations have become difficult or heated. But even if this woman you're taking a step back from isn't being a friend to you, you can still honor her dignity as the relationship evolves and ends.

Practically, that starts with not gossiping about her or your former friendship with your other friends. Although you might want to air your grievances with someone, especially if you're an external processer, venting about how the breakup went will not only be uncharitable — it'll actually leave you feeling worse.

"Contrary to popular notion, aggressive 'venting' doesn't relieve bad feelings, but fuels them. Studies show that blowing up, punching a pillow, yelling, or slamming doors makes you feel worse, not better," explains Gretchen Rubin, who writes on happiness and human nature. "If you're feeling angry or sad, instead of expressing negative emotions in a dramatic way, try to act the way you wish you felt by finding a calm way to express your feelings."[14] Intentionally saying "no" to gossip can also help a friend-group navigate the repercussions of two friends in the group calling it quits, despite the friend-group staying together. If there's a chance you'll still interact with the woman you used to be friends with, make it a goal to treat her with kindness and respect when you see her next. Don't spend the conversation asking her deep probing questions or giving her the in-depth low down of your life. Pretending as if nothing happened between you wouldn't honor the reality of your finished friendship. So don't ignore her, but keep things respectful, even if it means erring on the side of formal.

Another way to honor her dignity is to resist the urge to mentally relive your friendship with her, looking for all the things you wish you could change. There might be ways you could have communicated better and things you shouldn't have done, and the same could be said for her actions and words, too. In some cases, better communication and honesty up front in a relationship could have made a difference in the trajectory of a friendship. Sometimes that's not the reality, though. There are also deeper issues that could lead to a friendship crumbling that you have no control over. If you find yourself mentally replaying everything from your arguments to your good memories, work on surrendering them to the Lord in that moment. A friend recently shared a prayer by Reverend John Williamson that I've found incredibly helpful for breaking out of unhealthy thought spirals: "What has been done has been done; what has not been done has not been done; let it be." Honor yourself and her by surrendering even your memories and emotions to the Lord.

After a friendship breakup, it can be tempting to social-media-stalk her. It can start innocently enough, just a curiosity to see how she's doing. But that desire can lead to a morbid curiosity, or even the hope that you find out things aren't going well for her. Just like it's a good idea to unfollow your exes after a romantic relationship, take a step back and unfollow this woman on social media. By doing so, you're also giving yourself the space you need to process and heal from the end of the friendship. That's made harder when you're looking at her breakfast pictures and the quotes she shares.

Lastly, work toward forgiveness. If you haven't even formally started a friendship breakup, this can feel like a big step. I remember when I was struggling to forgive a woman who'd hurt me deeply, I took that struggle to a priest I trusted. He shared with me that I didn't have to start with praying for forgiveness. If that felt like too big of a step, I could start praying to want to pray for forgiveness. If forgiveness seems impossible even then, ask God for the grace to see this woman as he sees her. Forgiving her doesn't mean you have to forget everything that hurt you in the friendship. And forgiveness doesn't mean that you have to be friends with her again. But forgiveness is a necessary step when it comes to healing from a friendship that ended, whether you ended it or you were the friend who someone broke up with.

I'm not going to lie; friendship breakups will be a challenge. Striving for wholesome and authentic friendships in our lives isn't going to be easy. But if the friendship can grow to a point where it helps both of you become the women Christ created you to be, the challenge and discomfort is totally worth it.

Receiving the Gift of Authentic Friendship

The next time a friend offers to help you with something heavy that you're going through (the loss of a loved one, an illness in your family, a hard financial situation), accept their help humbly and thankfully.

Giving the Gift of Authentic Friendship

Have you been blessed by the gift of authentic friendship with women in your life? Write a list of those women, then spend the next few days praying for each one specifically by name. You could even reach out to each woman and ask her if there is any particular intention to keep in mind as you lift her up in prayer. If you have never experienced this type of soul-level friendship with the women in your life, spend time today bringing that desire to the Lord in prayer.

Real Talk *with* **Carolyn Shields**

Friendships in Seasons of Change

I peered over our backyard fence when the nun next door beckoned us closer. "This is Olivia," she said stepping aside, and this little skinny, bespectacled girl with a bob shyly waved. "She's your new neighbor."

I bolted inside. "Mom! MOM! Please don't make us play with her!"

We always laugh looking back at the first time we met each other at the age of eight. We grew up as neighbors for the rest of our childhood on the side of the mountain next to a lonesome sister whose name to us was always simply "Sister." Despite my first reaction of abhorrence (given only because I didn't want to share my playtime since my cousin was with us), we quickly became best friends. Childish adventures ensued — running wild in the woods while wearing capes Olivia made, putting miles on our bikes, hours of chess and dancing, and eventually we would work in the local café together, make trips to the nation's capital for its art galleries, and celebrate confirmations and graduations — but ultimately, we both had to go our separate ways.

Olivia headed to Franciscan University of Steubenville where she dove into journalism and philosophy. She eventually met her future spouse. I attended the local college where I dove into creating a website for theYoungCatholicWoman instead of studying for finals. I met a few now-exes. Olivia's and my paths were beginning to part as our adolescence merged with adulthood.

A few years after I graduated, I moved to West Philadelphia as Olivia made wedding plans.

We entered that awkward place so many girlfriends find themselves in, which is challenging for even the most solid of friendships: We were suddenly living out different vocations. These seasons can be especially hard when you feel called to the same vocation, and yet one is left watching as girlfriends walk down the aisle, change their last names, and eventually nurse their babies. Priorities shift, time is no longer her own, and many are left wanting their old friend back.

You don't have to be jealous or hurt for it to put a strain on your friendship. Given that we had lived in different states for years by this point, I wasn't grieving a dramatic change in our friendship, but I did notice we were simply no longer the same girls we were at the age of eight on that summer day. The years changed us, wisened us, sometimes in my case I wonder if it hardened me.

Struggling with debt, working for the Church on a small income, and living in the city had me seeking freelance work to keep my head above water. I began turning to theYoungCatholicWoman to supplement my income.

I spent hours building this ministry in my little apartment, in ripped jeans and old college t-shirts, as Olivia began her newly-wed Marine life. Our lives were looking more and more different from the shared summer days we had spent together.

One day when we were both home around Christmas, we stole time to visit a café while her one-year-old daughter napped, and I mentioned how I felt like God was asking me to publish a quarterly magazine.

"I would love to help with that."

I paused. Here was my lifelong friend with exactly the skills that could help, who I could trust, who was always able to handle my creative "brain dumps," whose patience and kindness was always needed ... but to do business with her? To ask of her a lot of work for no compensation? Didn't someone always say to never do business with family, which Olivia had been for a long time?

But ... I missed her. What if this could actually bring us together again?

I anxiously looked down at my black coffee as Olivia, always with a peaceful gaze, calmly sipped her almond milk caramel latte. I wondered, what if it would put a strain on our relationship? What if her husband didn't think she was being compensated fairly? What if we butted heads about the direction of the magazine? Up until this point, theYoungCatholicWoman was six years old and 99 percent a product of my own creation. I was always a lone wolf. I work better alone. I could avoid uncomfortable conversations, delegating, but as theYCW grew, I knew I could no longer do it by myself. And here was my best friend, offering to help — and she was a perfect fit. If God was truly asking me to create a magazine, I had to have help.

A few weeks later I called Olivia. "So … about the magazine. If you're serious, it could be really cool to go at it together." Today she is the print content manager and oversees a team of twelve writers to VIGIL, the only Catholic women's magazine currently on the market.

And once I could look past my fear, I quickly learned how working together has only served to help our relationship. We may still be living out different vocations and our lifestyles still look pretty different, but like marriage, maybe friendships need a common aim, especially when little else between you is similar. One day, God willing, I will have my own children and can partake in those conversations with her, but by us sharing in this ministry, the Lord has drawn us close again.

It's not necessarily always easy. We've had a hard conversation or two, but our filial love takes our mutual labor to strengthen what God has given us. Clarity, honesty, and gratitude, rather than shared memories, have become cornerstones in our relationship. Now our texts are not solely baby photos on her end and updates on life from me, but instead peppered with animated exchanges about the fruits of our labor.

We worked together serving coffee in our teens, and now we serve truth curated for the young Catholic woman … and I couldn't be more grateful.

Carolyn Shields is the Founder and Creative Director at theYoung-CatholicWoman & VIGIL magazine. She is the author of several books, including Visio Divina: Praying with Sacred Art. *She loves traveling, contemplating all things holy, and cornbread. Follow her on Instagram @carolyn.m.shields.*

4

Friendship in Seasons of Transition

I was never a Girl Scout, but my grandma was a troop leader and my mom and her sisters were all Girl Scouts for a while. I grew up singing all of the campfire songs, even though I didn't have a clue about how to actually start a campfire or pitch a tent. Despite my total lack of a green vest with little sewn-on badges, I'd bust out in those camp songs at the top of my lungs as I ran around my grandparents' house with my cousins. Between my expertise at singing the words to "Baby Bumble Bee" and my penchant for the Thin Mint cookies that my grandparents kept in their freezer on a regular basis, there's no question that I could have been an honorary scout.

I frequently still get the words from the official Girl Scout songbook stuck in my head. Every time I navigate a season of change or transition in life and those changes affect my friendships with the women who I'm blessed to call friends, the words of the Girl Scout song "Make New Friends" plays on repeat in my brain: "Make new friends and keep the old, / one is silver and the other, gold . . . you help me, and I'll help you, / and together we will see it through."

Now you may never have taken the Girl Scout promise, experienced a middle-school camping trip, or knocked on your neighbor's door and explained the difference between Shortbread and Thanks-A-Lots. However, you more than likely know exactly what it's like to try to make new friends while also trying your very best to keep in touch with old ones. And you know that the beauty and goodness of authentic sisterhood far outweighs the value of silver or gold. But how can we practically juggle making new friends, keeping old friends, and navigating change in our lives without everything falling down around us? Let's start by talking about what it means to keep old friends, then we'll talk about how to make new ones.

Our lives are incredibly seasonal. Many of us experience a season of singleness, where we're able to learn more about who we are as daughters of God and lean into our feminine genius through studies, work, and developing hobbies and interests. Then there are seasons of discernment, where we enter an intentional journey of finding out how specifically the Lord is calling us to pursue the universal call to holiness. If you're called to marriage, you may also experience the gift of physical or adoptive maternity as a fruit of that vocation — which can leave you feeling like you're in a never-ending revolving door of seasonal shifts as your children develop and grow (and as you develop and grow in your own maternity!). But we also experience different seasons in workplaces and careers, in situations like moving across the country, or even across town, as daughters as our parents age, and even more as we age ourselves.

Not all of us will experience each and every one of these different seasons, and there's no rule to say in what order we'll encounter them. You're also not required to move through all of these seasons to live a full life. However, despite what kind of change you're experiencing in your life today or the season of life that you're in, one thing is always true: Our friendships with other women are always impacted by these transitions. We've already talked about examining your heart for friendship and defining authentic friendship; now let's focus on the impact of external changes on your friendships.

In college, I was one of the last of my friend group to graduate, so many of my friends moved onto the next stage of life while I was still knee-deep in lecture notes and finals. And while I was one of the last in my friend group to go on a date in college, I was one of the first of us to get married. Then, I was the friend who moved away with my new husband. Among our new friends in a new city, I was one of the first to have children. I've not been a total rockstar in navigating these different changes in life or friendship. In fact, most of the thoughts I'll share with you here I've learned from the school of friendship mistakes. You may be going through a season of transition yourself, or you might be witnessing and accompanying a dear friend who is going through change and seeing that impact your relationship with her. So, if you're struggling to navigate transition with grace, pull up a seat and let me pour you another cup of coffee. You're in good company and I'm here to grow right alongside you.

Whether you're experiencing a season of change kickstarted by new jobs, cross-country moves, or vocational discernments, let's take time together to examine the unique challenges and joys of the different transitions that can impact friendship. At the end of the chapter, we'll touch on some universal principles for navigating any season of transition.

Friendship After You Flip Your Tassel

During college, despite how sleep-deprived and caffeine-high I often was during those four years, friendships blossomed naturally. I shared classes with many dear friends, studying history and bonding over rough assignments from our favorite professors. Off campus, I made fast friends with the women I met at the Catholic campus center, joining them for Bible studies and heart-to-hearts at our local coffee shop.

In many ways, my time in college reminded me of religious life. Hang with me — I know that many of our collegiate experiences are a far cry from monks or nuns living with a vow of silence. But like women religious, the women I met in college and I shared an "horarium," a regular daily schedule and way of life. Even if we were in classes at different times or worked different jobs between lectures and labs, we were all living in the same season together. We gathered for common meals in the cafeteria or at our favorite sandwich shop. Nights were spent poring over sources in the library or lounging on dorm beds, digging through a pile of homework together. My friends and I would gather for Mass on the weekend and then relax before starting the next week.

But despite feeling like we'd never get through that foreign language class, or that our college careers were never-ending, those four years flew by. Before we knew it, my friends and I were marching across the stage to "Pomp and Circumstance," praying that we wouldn't trip down the stairs in front of the entire college. As soon as we were handed that diploma, our shared way of life disappeared.

The women in my major program went onto grad school or embarked on their first jobs. Friends I'd sat across the aisle from at Mass moved across the country. In the blink of an eye, life happened to all of us. Even when we managed to coordinate a lunch — which often left me feeling the need to put together a spreadsheet of schedules to find a common time where we were all back in town and free to meet up — we all were continuing to grow in our interests and different seasons of life. New jobs, hobbies, and families made our old friendships seem like a distant memory.

But despite all of these changes, maintaining college friendships isn't impossible. The first thing to keep in mind is the reality of your state of life. Don't get me wrong, there are still times I wish I was back in college. Most of the time that desire ends as soon as I remember all-nighters and final exams, but I look back on those days of camaraderie fondly. But the reality is that many of my college friends are spread throughout the United States and I'm more likely to see them on my Instagram feed than I am to run into them at the grocery store or in a women's small group. Our relationships have evolved and matured after graduation, and those kinds of changes are normal. Instead of pining for what once was in our friendships, accepting the reality of our lives allows us all to continue growing, discovering more about who God created us to be. Our time in college together is filled with good memories, and I'm excited to see what God has in store for us in this season of new careers, vocation discernments, marriages, and growing families, too.

If you don't live near the friends you connected with in classrooms and cafeterias, make connecting a priority. A quick email to a friend sharing an article that made you think of her can make those miles between you seem insignificant. I know other friends who connect to their long-distance besties by watching movies together or keeping up their streak of an online game. Another one of my friends creates a fun Christmas card every year, updating people on her new adventures. Even if she hasn't touched base with someone that year, sometimes that Christmas card sparks a fun conversation and point of connection around the holidays.

Because you probably won't be running into each other on a regular basis, that means that you have to be intentional and committed to creating opportunities where you can continue to deepen your friendship. You'll have to accept the fact that friendships after your collegiate days draw to a close are going to take a lot more effort than they did back when you saw your best friend in class every day, or called her your neighbor.

Friendships after this loss of convenient commonality require intentionality and effort. But if both you and your friends are committed to valuing the friendship despite your new differences in location or season of life, your friendship can continue to grow and mature.

You Don't Have to Choose Between Friendship and Romance

A new romantic relationship is incredibly exciting. It can mean hours spent with a man you're learning to love, endless late-night conversations, and adventures with a new companion. But many of us have had the experience of looking up from a new relationship only to realize that we haven't caught up with our girlfriends in what seems like forever. They might have started to put together a search party. Likewise, many of us have been on the receiving end of this situation — when friends who we used to see regularly become invisible once a guy comes on the scene.

If your relationship takes a serious turn and you begin to discern a lifelong vocation together, your priorities will naturally shift — but that doesn't mean that friendship with women is inherently incompatible with a romantic relationship.

The key here (again!) is intentionality and communication — are you sensing a theme?

If you were the invisible woman in the friendship, don't be afraid to ask for forgiveness and propose a fresh start with your friends. It's not realistic to expect that everything will stay the same as your schedules shift and your busyness increases, but giving each other the chance to share expectations can help everyone involved avoid disappointment.

Because you're sharing your schedule with your significant other, time with your friends might need to become something you intentionally schedule instead of just waiting for it to happen. Make time in your calendar on the regular to touch base with your friends so that their value to you translates into some real-life, practical get-togethers. Monday evenings could be a time you send a catch-up text if you weren't able to see each other over the weekend. Or maybe you pencil in a regular happy hour with the ladies so that a chance to catch up is always on the calendar.

You can strive for this intentionality whether you're the one who is dating or the one who is watching her friends discern their vocations. And if you're good friends with someone who is falling off the radar after starting into a new romantic relationship, be honest with her if you've felt alone or left out since her relationship status changed.

Remember that your regular catch-up time doesn't have to be a special occasion. You can (and should!) invite your friends into your everyday activities. Maybe you can hit the gym together in the mornings, go grocery shopping together, or set a date for a book club so that you can work through your to-read list together. If your close friends don't live in the same town, you can meet for a digital friend date over a video chat, or take your book club or game night virtual via an app like Zoom or Discord.

Most importantly, remember that your romantic relationship and your friendships don't have to exist in different spheres, never to cross paths. An integrated life, where your relationship and friendships coexist, can be more relaxing and natural for everyone involved. Start by hosting your boyfriend and friends for a game night or dinner. Your significant other will get to know the women who you love and trust, and your girlfriends will be able to witness your romantic relationship blossom — and warn of any red flags you may be blind to. If the women in your life are in relationships, too, you can always schedule a few double dates so that everyone can get to know each other.

Romantic relationships are an incredible gift, but they're not a replacement for sisterhood. Just like we can't assume that the women in our lives will bring total fulfillment to all of our desires, the men in our lives can't fill those shoes either, and even though you are spending so much time together, you can't expect him to fill the place of all of your valuable female friendships. You'll end up disappointed if you believe that your boyfriend (or fiancé! or husband!) will fill your desire for the feminine genius.

To put it bluntly, your boyfriend isn't a woman.

He'll complement your feminine genius by his masculine gifts and talents, but he won't be able to fulfill your desire for feminine friendship.

When you spend quality time with your significant other while also intentionally spending time with the women in your life, you'll reach a more balanced relational life which will benefit everyone. You'll be able to get to know your boyfriend without expecting him to be your one and only friend, and you'll be able to give and receive the gift of friendship with the women in your life and not leave them in the dust at the first sign of a diamond ring.

When One of You Does Put a Ring on It

I have so many fond memories of wedding receptions when my friends and I would hit the dance floor at the first few notes of Beyoncé's "Single Ladies." There wasn't a ring in sight for us, and that shared experience — combined with some slick dance moves — made for great evenings.

But gradually, our men started putting rings on it, and before we knew it, we were dancing at our own wedding receptions, surrounded by friends who were married, engaged, dating, and single. Vocational discernment will impact your friendships, there's no getting around it. But despite the intentional navigation required, sisterhood in this new season of life will continue to be a gift you and I both give and receive, rings on our fingers or not.

A recent study of 3,000 married couples revealed that those who included more than two hundred guests at their wedding celebration were 92 percent less likely to be divorced than the case study reference point.[1] Now, the number of tables couples have set up at their reception isn't a guarantee of marital success. After all, you and I both probably know some stellar couples who got married in the midst of a world pandemic and had to narrow their guest list down from hundreds to ten, including themselves and the priest. But having a community surrounding you as you embark on the adventure of marriage is an incredible blessing that can translate into some real marriage success. However, if you ditch your friends as soon as you pull away in your car that they painted "just married" all over, it won't matter how many of them were dancing at your wedding reception. Long after the wedding bells stop pealing, this community will take intentional investment.

If you're part of a married couple, strive to integrate your friendships into your vocation. Host your friends — single, dating, and married alike — for dinners and game nights. Invite them into your home, no matter how unorganized or Pinterest-worthy it might be. (We'll talk about this more in a later chapter.) But also make time in your calendar for your friends as individuals. Remember that your spouse isn't a woman, and so penciling in time for drinks or dinner with just the ladies is something that will be a gift to everyone involved.

While some of the friendships from your single-lady dancing days will translate naturally into friendships that you share with your spouse, some of the women in your life can be just your friends — that's okay. Take each friendship on a case-by-case scenario and ask the Holy Spirit to help you navigate how your vocation will impact each one. Even if some friendships are more your friends as an individual than as a couple, don't be afraid to talk about each one with your spouse. Have an intentional conversation together about the importance of friendship in your lives both as a couple and as individuals.

Marriage also brings some natural shifts in conversation topics with friends and a need for intentionality and awareness of boundaries. When you get married, your spouse becomes the recipient of your deepest emotional vulnerability and intimacy. While you may have called a girlfriend first with good news or dialed her number to vent about a hard day at work, now your husband is your go-to person. In the Sacrament of Matrimony, you become a total gift of yourself to him in a way that wasn't even possible with your girlfriends. But this switching of allegiances means that conversations with your friends might change, and some topics might need more intentional discernment before sharing. Your best friend does not need to know everything about your husband, especially things he's entrusted to you alone. Your marriage doesn't need to be a secret or an off-limits conversation topic, but there's a problem if you're talking more *about* your husband and an issue you're struggling with in your marriage to your best friend and not talking about that issue *with* your spouse. If you're friends with someone who has a tendency to gossip and vent about their spouse, gently ask them if they've talked with their spouse about the problem they're experiencing. Your goal is to champion their marriage together, not to pick sides and pledge loyalty to your friend, casting blame on her spouse and making her question her decision to marry him.

As a married woman, your vocation is the way you encounter the Lord, and it's your mission in life to journey to heaven with your spouse. If there's a conflict between your friendship and your vocation, your marriage has to come first. That isn't to say that friendships are unnecessary, they just need to be rightly ordered. If you're married, it's important to invest in friendships with women who are living in the same season. These women are able to speak into the nitty-gritty experience of pursuing holiness in a vocation with another human being. There's something truly beautiful about being able to sit down in conversation with another married woman and discuss topics like practicing natural family planning or navigating extended family relationships.

At the same time, spend time with your single friends and take genuine interest in their lives. They don't need your pity; they need your friendship. And you need their friendship, too. This is a two-way street, remember? You can give your single friends the gift of truly being yourself in your marriage and in your family. Invite them into your daily life, whether that's a standing invitation to Saturday brunch or a place in your pew at Mass so they don't have to sit alone if they don't want to. Your authenticity in this invitation can help your single friends recognize the realities of married life, which can help them realize that although married life is not Disney-perfect, there is so much beauty in the joys of marriage and grace in the struggles. Your home can become a place for your single friends to land and simply be, and your dining room table or front room couch can become a place for them to enter into family and community life. When I was a single woman, especially when I was far away from home, good married friends who invited me along on trips to the lake or summer barbeques were such a gift — one I strive to give to my single friends now that I'm the one who is married.

If you're a single woman and your friend is married, you can give her the gift of sensitivity and grace in your friendship together. Maybe she isn't able to respond to a text as fast as she used to since her kids are nap-striking or her husband came home from work early. By adjusting your expectations and being patient, you are able to communicate that your friendship is worth it, even if it looks different these days. One of my best friends is a single woman and we've reconnected over hobbies we used to share when we were both single. She started a book club and invited me into it, rekindling good conversations about our favorite characters and plot lines, and giving me the encouragement I needed to carve out space in my week for reading a good book, even though that's not a pastime my husband and I share the same excitement for. But she's also invited me into new hobbies that we can share as friends even though our seasons of life are mismatched — everything from floral arranging classes at our local community center, to murder mystery night parties that she's invited both me and my husband to. She knows I can't say yes to every invitation, since some fun opportunities collide with family in town or the need for a date night with my husband. But her kind and continual invitations remind me that she still treasures our friendship, even if it looks different than it did before I discerned a vocation of marriage.

Shared calendars, the good and holy weight of the Sacrament of Marriage, and the logistics of navigating a vocation will change some of the practical day-to-day realities of sisterhood. But whether you're the newlywed or the friend catching the bouquet and rocking those Beyoncé moves, a new season can bring with it so much grace and fruit.

Growing in Friendship as Families Grow

For a season of my life, I was afraid to invite friends with kids over to my house. I didn't have a tub of toys in my front room and I hadn't child-proofed the bathrooms. I wasn't even sure what their kids would do while the adults were chatting.

But then I was blessed with my own littles here on earth and that totally shifted. My house overflowed with toys and I honestly regretted the times that I'd shied away from inviting my friends with kids into my house. I'd missed out on receiving the gift of their friendship because I was too worried about what their kids would be doing in the hour that we were catching up. I learned that kids are pretty good at figuring out unique ways to entertain themselves. These days, I strive to invite a variety of friends into our home, regardless of whether little people trot in alongside them or not.

If you're a mom with friends who aren't in a season of mothering, don't be afraid to invite them for a warm cup of coffee and a seat on your couch (after you clear away the Magnatiles and board books). Again, friendship doesn't stop being a gift to give and receive once kids come onto the scene. Your friends who aren't jug-gling diaper bags and drop-off schedules can give you the beauty of adult conversations around deeper topics than mashed bananas. Be intentional with taking interest in your friends' lives, interests, hobbies, and desires. Just like you love talking about your baby's new developments and sleeping patterns, she loves talking about her hobbies, so give her space to unfold and be comfortable around you despite your different seasons.

Meanwhile, if you're the friend who doesn't have children and is dodging Legos on the way to the guest bathroom, your friend's witness to the beauty of this season of mothering can be a gift for you, too. Her motherhood offers you a real, tangible example of the maternal aspects of the feminine genius. Witnessing her mother her children can also help you recognize the realities of parenting, which can come in handy in the future. You might think of her parenting when you are wrestling your own toddlers, or it could equip you to encounter the kids in your life with more patience and grace. So, reach out to that sleep deprived mom-friend of yours and ask how you can grow in friendship with her and her expand-ing family. And while friendship with women is amazing, there's also something pretty magical about friendship with five-year-olds who share their school projects, latest obsessions, and quirky jokes with you.

Regardless of whether you're the one with or without kids, get comfortable being flexible with the changes in what friend dates look like. They might be scheduled around naptimes and involve a lot more coffee. But continue to include friends in regular invita-tions, even if you have an inkling that not everyone will be able to say yes right now. Little by little, it'll get easier to say yes and thrive in this new, messy — and literally sticky — season of friendship.

When You're Waving Goodbye in the Rearview Mirror

In 2017, I was newly married and in a brand-new city. As I unpacked boxes and opened wedding gifts, I started to grieve my old friendships. Some of my friends had also packed their cars to the brim and headed off to new jobs, new schools, and new homes, but some of my friends still lived in my hometown. I was trying to form new friendships in this new city while also trying to stay in touch with the old friends who still called our college town home.

When I would browse social media on Monday mornings, photos of friends who hadn't moved away spending time together would float through my feed and I battled feelings of jealousy and regret. I wanted to be included, even though I knew that was physically impossible because of the distance. I worried that since I wasn't living in the same town as many of my friends were, they'd forget about me and go on to form even deeper friendships while I was left behind. I thought that there was no way I could invest in new friendships while I mourned the what-was of the friendships I had in college. If I made new friends, wouldn't I be abandoning my old friends?

It can be hard to see your friend spending time with others after you become long-distance. It's okay to recognize that this will sting a little bit. But instead of buying into jealousy, rejoice that your friend is encountering authentic friendships in her life. Just because she is having someone over for the game night that used to be just for you two doesn't mean that your friendship is forgotten or replaced. And just like she isn't replacing you, you aren't replacing her by being present in your current situation in your new digs, either, or abandoning her by investing in new friendships with women. In fact, when you both are living in the present moment and striving for an integrated life, you'll have a greater capacity to share yourself with others and receive their friendship, whether they live in your city or miles away.

Regardless of whether you're unpacking your suitcase or waving goodbye to the friend driving off into the sunset, long distance friendships can be challenging. If you've moved far away and crossed time zones, maintaining your friendships can be full of sticky situations. Worrying whether your friend will still be at work (or asleep!) when you call can make contacting each other pretty difficult sometimes. And even if you're in the same time zone, not knowing the other person's schedule can lead to some impressive games of phone tag.

Although technology makes it easy to leave messages for the recipient's convenience, there's something to be said about intentional communication. If you're sick of sending out text messages and never knowing if now is a good time, may I suggest an old-fashioned remedy? Snail mail.

Taking time out of your schedule to write a letter, postcard, or just a quick note to your long-distance friend is a great way to foster intentional conversation. And if there's one thing adult life has taught me, it's that getting something besides a bill in the mailbox can make my whole day! Send your long-distance friend a quick note in the mail just to let her know that you're thinking of her and miss her. But she doesn't have to live hundreds of miles away in order for you to pick up the pen and send her a quick note. One of my dear friends from college took an intentional step away from social media and has used her newfound free time to write letters to her family and friends, even if they live down the street. And another one of my friends who lives just one town over always remembers to send me a postcard during her international travels. Seeing something in the mail from either of them is a tangible reminder of the gift of our friendship. And let's be honest, even if you live in the same city, coordinating time for a friend date can prove challenging between work schedules and commitments. I'm a big proponent of snail mail, regardless of how many miles are between the mailboxes.

Finally, one more practical thing to improve your communication with long-distance friends: Be intentional with the way you share big news. There's something truly beautiful about connecting over a Skype coffee date or phone call to share big news, whether that's news to celebrate or news to mourn. And there's nothing that hurts more than seeing a huge life update in a good friend's life on Facebook before hearing it from them personally. Whether chosen consciously or subconsciously, the way you communicate big life events and the order of people who you share that news with reveals to others the value that you place in your friendship and their closeness to you. When Joseph and I found out, the spring after we were married, that we were expecting Marion, we wanted to make sure to reach out to friends and family personally. And when we found out just eight weeks later that Marion wasn't going to be born on this side of heaven, those same friends cried alongside us and journeyed with us throughout the stages of grief.

Whether it's an engagement, pregnancy announcement, new job or new house, make sure to intentionally contact your close friends before posting that update on Facebook. Make sure that those who are nearest to your heart will be able to celebrate with you before the entire world finds out.

Your friends who are separated by miles and miles don't have to become just Facebook friends who you see every once in a while, when they show up on your feed. With a lot of intentionality and communication, these friendships can grow despite the distance. (We'll talk in depth about digital friendships, new and old, later on.)

When a Friend Leaves the Faith

According to Pew Research Center, about half (52 percent) of all adults living in the United States who were raised Catholic have left the Catholic Church at some point in their lives.[2] And while some of those who leave Catholicism return eventually, many don't come back. With numbers like those, there's a chance that you know a friend who has left the Catholic Faith. In fact, stepping away from Catholicism for a season may even be part of your own past.

Witnessing a friend leaving the Church can be incredibly challenging, especially if your shared faith was an important part of your friendship. If your friend shares the story of why she's leaving Catholicism, you could find yourself grieving for her and what she's gone through. You may question whether you could have said or done something different that could have impacted her decision, or find yourself angry that this is even happening. Or you might wonder how to broach the topic of her faith journey with her, wondering if you need all the answers before beginning a conversation.

If you're in a season of transition with a friend who is stepping away from the Catholic Church, the most important thing you can do is simply be present and listen to her story. "A woman's soul is designed ... to be a shelter in which other souls may unfold," St. Teresa Benedicta of the Cross wrote. "The soul of woman must therefore be expansive and open to all human beings; it must be quiet so that no small weak flame will be extinguished by stormy winds; warm so as to not benumb fragile buds; clear, so that no vermin will settle in dark corners and recesses; self-contained, so that no invasions from without can imperil the inner life; empty of itself, in order that extraneous life may have room in it; finally, mistress of itself and also of its body, so that the entire person is readily at the disposal of every call."[3]

Your gift of friendship in this season is to create an environment for your friend where she can be herself and be truly seen and heard. You don't have to have all the answers to listen to her share her struggles. Although she may be wrestling with some hard topics, more than likely she isn't looking for you to give her the answers. She's looking for your friendship — an authentic friendship that wants the best for her and desires to see her grow in holiness.

Remember the old adage that people don't care about how

much you know until they know how much you care. Take time to truly listen to her experience, not so that you can interject with quotes from the *Catechism* to prove her wrong, but so that she knows someone is listening and honestly cares about her experience.

At the same time, you can be honest with her about your own experience with Catholicism. You don't have to hide your love of the Faith, despite the messiness that is part of being in a Church filled with human beings who forget the Lord's call to holiness. Don't shy away from conversations about why the Faith matters in your own life, whether that's mentioning how your adoration hour was or sharing a podcast or book recommendation with her when she asks. Navigating tough topics can also be an incredible chance to share vulnerably about your own experience with the Faith. Maybe you, too, have struggled with certain teachings of the Church and can give witness to why you're still Catholic yourself.

And above all, pray for her. That might seem like a trite closing thought, but it's not. Prayer is immeasurably important in our friendships, and sometimes, when someone is making a decision we would do anything we could to change, prayer is the first (and best!) place we can land. God loves your friend immeasurably more than you do, and taking this experience to prayer can help you remember that first and foremost, your friend is a daughter of God, no matter her choices.

Whatever Change Looks Like, Keep These Things in Mind

Maybe I've spoken about the exact season of change you're experiencing with your friends. Or perhaps you're reaching the end of this chapter frustrated that something about your specific circumstances wasn't included in these few pages. But whether your experience was mentioned in detail here or not, there are some universal principles of navigating transition with friends that can apply to any situation.

First, it's important to remember to navigate seasons of change with patience and compassion for everyone involved, yourself included. When tensions are high, it's tempting to assume that the worst-case scenario is the reality of your situation. But before jumping to conclusions and assuming the worst of the situation and your friends, remember to operate out of total generosity. Assume the best, not the worst. Remember, transitions are difficult for everyone involved.

To avoid miscommunication, lean toward overcommunication in seasons of change. Share your expectations and how you think the situation will impact your friendship. And don't forget to be honest. It might seem like sugarcoating your struggle or not mentioning everything on your heart is helpful but the opposite is true. Communicating with clarity and kindness can make all the difference in a friendship surviving a season of change. Talk about the way you're experiencing this season out loud with your friends. When you communicate early and often with your friends, you'll be able to address signs of conflict right away instead of running the risk of little miscommunications becoming large, ugly, festering wounds.

Regardless of what season of change and transition you're navigating, always remember to surrender everything to the Lord: your friendships, your new connections with women in your life, the awkwardness of honest conversations, and the grieving of what once was with your friends. And, as hard as it can be sometimes (all the time?), be patient with yourself and with your friends as you grow in your ability to love each other and honor the gift of friendship in seasons of change.

You're not the first or only woman to struggle with growth and change in a friendship. Even the saints knew what it was like to be frustrated that those friendships didn't look like the ideal quite yet. When she was instructing the nuns who lived in the Carmelite convents she founded, St. Teresa of Ávila penned *The Way of Perfection*. She dedicated an entire chapter to speaking about what spiritual love and feminine friendship looked like in practice within the walls of the communities. In that chapter, she speaks into the natural time it takes to grow and be perfected in loving others, writing,

"This spiritual love is the kind of love I would desire us to have. Even though in the beginning it is not so perfect, the Lord will gradually perfect it. Let us begin by using the suitable means, for, even though the love bears with it some natural tenderness, no harm will be done provided this tenderness is shown toward all."

Seasons of change can bring challenges — no doubt about that. They're not perfect, and they can be downright frustrating. But those same seasons of transition can also strengthen your friendship and encourage you to grow in the way you intentionally give and receive sisterhood like nothing else. Be gentle with your friends, and be gentle with yourself. It's through these seasons of change, as messy as they are, that the Lord is perfecting your ability to give and receive friendship.

Receiving the Gift of Friendship
in Seasons of Transition

If you're navigating a change and see that change impacting your friendships with the women in your life, take time to communicate your hopes and dreams for your friendship after the season settles down. Then, take time to listen to your friends' expectations and see how you can best serve her in this season.

Giving the Gift of Friendship
in Seasons of Transition

If you're friends with a woman who is navigating a season of change right now, strive to operate out of a place of maximum generosity and assume the best of her. Instead of resenting the change she's going through, ask her if there are any ways you can help make this season smoother for her.

Friendships That Overcome Comparison

T en years ago, I stood just inside the doorway of a lovely, two-story colonial. I was a young mom of two in the middle of figuring out what in the world we were doing for kindergarten. Our parish homeschool group was holding a meeting for Little Flowers, a club for young Catholic girls.

The home had a front porch and a light-filled entryway, so different from the tiny townhouse we called home. Other moms and daughters were gathered in the living room around a well-loved coffee table. Wishing I had her confidence (or lack of social awareness, maybe), I watched my bright and quirky five-year-old take off through the crowd.

I didn't follow her — at least not with anything other than my eyes. I stood rooted to the spot, a chubby, wild-grinned six-month-old strapped to my back in an Ergo. I sucked in my middle in an ill-fated attempt to hide what I thought was a generous muffin top.

"Please don't look at me. Please don't look at me. I'll just hide in plain sight over here," I thought. My desperate plea didn't work, of course — I was letting all the cold air in. An older mom smiled and ushered me through the door. I scanned the room, eyes cataloging the other women in attendance. My eyes fell on Erica — she was trim, tanned, and charismatic.

My face flamed and my shoulders pulled inward. Erica smiled and tweaked the ball cap on her head. This wasn't Erica's house; she'd brought her daughter to Little Flowers just like I had. But at that moment, I felt sure I didn't belong. I was frumpy (I thought); I knew I was sleep-deprived and could barely hold a conversation. I was jealous and compared myself to every other mom there, especially Erica. She looked so put together. She looked like everything I did not.

God has quite a sense of humor, however. I wrote off any sort of friendship with Erica only for the two of us to be thrust together six months later in the parochial school parking lot. I still felt inferior — so inferior — but apparently, Erica didn't give any of it a second thought. We got to know each other while chasing toddlers through the school prayer garden.

Erica's my best friend, my ride-or-die companion, our bond almost a decade old now. Why am I telling you all this? Because the truth is, I'm a master at envy and comparison. Chalk it up to my pride, my melancholic-leaning temperament, or my experiences with mean girls; whatever the root is, it's made female friendships really hard. So hard, in fact, that each of my strong adult relationships has a history of one-sided, comparison-induced drama.

My roommates Leslie and Emily in college, my dear friend Erica in motherhood. I pushed each of these women away because I thought I wasn't good enough. They were outgoing. I was the shy one. They were confident. I wanted to run and hide. They were beautiful and engaging and the kind of souls who easily draw people to them. From my vantage point on comparison corner, I was decidedly not. It's a good thing God's mercy is endless, however, because despite my best sabotage efforts, these women became my friends.

Em and Leslie carried me back to God after a period of dark, desperate depression. Together, Erica and I have weathered infant loss, troubles with school and academic decisions, ill-advised home renovation projects, panic attacks, and a global pandemic just to start. She's the woman who showed up at my house with a drill in hand so I didn't have to assemble my kids' trampoline all by myself. (I had texted her a brief: "Do you think I can do this?" She said, "Of course you can. I'm still coming to help.")

God sent these women to refine me, to help make me the woman he designed. My tendency to compare myself with others nearly cost me those opportunities because it was a desolation. Comparison is not a thought of God. What is comparison among women? It is a thief of grace. It is a disruptor of dignity. It is a dampener of peace and trust. Where friendship among women offers a sisterhood of grace and companionship, comparison puts up walls and leaves you shivering in the doorway. Let go of it, and let your heart accept the grace-filled possibility. It's so much warmer, so much better, among friends.

Ginny Kochis is a Catholic wife and mother of three differently wired children. Through her website and online communities, Ginny provides practical support and prayerful encouragement to Catholic moms of exceptional kids. Get in touch with Ginny at her online home, www.notsoformulaic.com.

5

Conquering Competition and Comparison with Celebration

"You really should be doing more ab workouts. Or just workouts in general," I think to myself as I scroll past my friend who is passionate about healthy eating and intentional exercise.

"If you took more time to get ready in the morning, your makeup could look like hers," I mutter as I see a new makeup tutorial from a friend who finds joy trying new makeup trends.

"Your thrift store tank tops do not even come close to her wardrobe," I sigh, shuffling through my closet as I watch an IGTV video of a friend sharing her outfits for the upcoming season.

"She's so much holier than I am," is what I think as I settle in for a hurried prayer time while seeing a friend share a picture from her gorgeous prayer corner.

"She has everything I want and she looks so happy," I assume as I close Instagram to make breakfast.

In just a few minutes, from the time I've rolled out of bed to when I've landed in the kitchen for my first cup of coffee, my stress levels and discontent have skyrocketed. That's not a surprising or isolated experience, since 86 percent of Americans admit that they "constantly or often check their emails, texts, and social media accounts" according to a recent survey.[1] And if those constant levels of interaction are negative, like those that lead to competition and comparison in our friendships, our constant checking in on others' lives can lead to higher levels of depression and anxiety.[2]

But the comparison doesn't end when the phone is powered down. From the women at Target to the women who sit across the aisle from me at Mass on Sunday, there's no shortage of opportunities for me to hold my story up and criticize it in comparison to my perception of others.

Do you know the feeling? Maybe the success of your coworker not only makes you green with jealousy, but also leaves you wondering if you'll ever be enough. Listening to your friend's journey towards healthy body image can cause you to spiral down a negative rabbit hole, critiquing every food and lifestyle choice you've ever made. Your sister mentioning the number on her paycheck makes you squirm, wishing you didn't know she made that much more than you, despite all of your hard work. Or maybe watching the mom in front of you at Mass makes you wonder if you're the only one struggling to round up squashed cheerios and stop seemingly constant crying.

If you struggle with comparing your story, talents, closet, family, passions, hobbies, joys, struggles, body shape, or relationship with God to those of other women, you're in good company. Many of us count likes on our Instagram posts, base our self-worth on our appearance according to some elusive standard, or wonder if we're a failure if our life doesn't look like that of our favorite influencer or the women in our small group.

With all of the opportunities for comparison around us, it could seem like the antidote is becoming a hermit and squirreling yourself away in a cave where no women (or Instagram!) can be seen. But the answer isn't to run away. It's actually the opposite, something that could seem a little counterintuitive at first. Oh, and it involves confetti.

Turning Toward Celebration

In Luke's Gospel, we meet Saint Elizabeth, Our Lady's cousin. After the Annunciation, Mary goes to meet Elizabeth in the hill country to be with her during the last few months of Elizabeth's pregnancy. When Mary arrives, Elizabeth's greeting captures the authentic and immense joy that we find when we are able to fully rejoice over the gifts God has given to each of us.

When Elizabeth hears Mary entering the house and listens to the words she shares in greeting, John the Baptist leaps in her womb. The Holy Spirit fills Elizabeth to the brim with authentic joy and she exclaims, "Blessed are you among women, and blessed is the fruit of your womb! And why is this granted me, that the mother of my Lord should come to me? For behold, when the voice of your greeting came to my ears, the child in my womb leaped for joy. And blessed is she who believed that there would be a fulfillment of what was spoken to her from the Lord" (Lk 1:42–45).

At the Visitation, both Mary and Elizabeth celebrate the gifts of the Lord in each other's lives, and give the full glory to God for the miracles they're both experiencing. Elizabeth was well beyond childbearing years, but she was pregnant with a son who was destined to prepare the Israelite people for the coming Messiah. Mary was also pregnant. The power of the Most High had overshadowed her and the baby she bore in her womb was the long-awaited Messiah himself.

What *don't* we see in this encounter? Elizabeth doesn't express feelings of inadequacy or compare her story to Mary's, resenting that her cousin was chosen to bear Christ. Mary doesn't gloat over her pregnancy with the Son of God himself. Instead, both give to each other generously and are able to rejoice fully together. Mary travels across miles of hill country to be with Elizabeth during the last three uncomfortable months of pregnancy, all while experiencing the first trimester herself. Elizabeth exclaims about the honor it is to receive Mary and the Christ child in her home, and opens up her home in generous hospitality to Mary for the next three months.

They're able to do this because each of them is confident in their identity as God's daughters and in his plan for their lives. Instead of worrying over whose experience overshadows the other, or who is more blessed, each of them turns their focus outward to the other and upwards toward God. Instead of falling prey to comparison or competition, Mary and Elizabeth are incredible models of a culture of celebration — and that's the attitude and culture that will make it possible for us to battle comparison and competition, starting today.

Celebrating the Other in True Friendship

Every single one of us is a unique, beautiful, and beloved daughter of God. We each have a feminine genius, a particular expression of the femininity the Lord has blessed us with, to encounter him and share his joy and goodness with others. Jealousy of the gifts and talents we witness not only stirs up resentment and competition in our friendships, it also causes us to miss out on the talents the Lord has blessed us with. We get so wrapped up in wishing the Lord had given us her exact gifts that we forget what he has given us. Comparison blinds us, leaving us with a skewed vision of the woman we're comparing ourselves to, but also of ourselves and the woman

God has created us to be.

Jealousy and comparison create a false image of who another woman is, as we make assumptions about her experiences and story. "If only we wanted to be happy, it would be easy; but we want to be happier than other people, which is almost always difficult, since we think them happier than they are," Charles de Montesquieu wrote. When we compare our stories, we idolize another's experience and begin to question the goodness of God in our lives. But it's all feelings that are based on what we perceive, not on a true reality of encountering each woman as a daughter of God, and giving and receiving friendship with them.

What if we strove for true friendship? Created a culture where we celebrated another's triumphs and joys instead of secretly wishing for the same things in our lives? Instead of feeling the pressure to keep up with her and prove to her (to ourselves?) that we are just as good if not better, we'd be free to simply learn about her story and accompany her on her journey. We'd be able to look up to the woman we admire instead of looking down or looking at her.

I don't know about you, but that kind of world seems much more joyful and peaceful than the one where I'm always worried that someone has it better than I do, or where I have to prove something to the women I know and love.

How can we embrace celebration and reject comparison and competition? Let's start by asking ourselves a few questions.

Who Is She?

It's easy to compare ourselves to other women, especially women who we don't know all that well. That isn't to say that our intimate friendships are automatically free of comparison or competition — I wish! But when you don't know the whole story of another woman's season or situation, it's tempting to fill in the blanks — which leaves you with a false perception. If we know all about how she styles her hair in the morning, the route she takes on her morning walks, the last recipe she tried for dinner, and her go-to coffee order, we know all there is to know about her, right? Wrong.

The woman you're comparing yourself to is a human being. She's a beloved daughter of God. If her front room looks immaculate, clean, and clutter-free, there's a good chance she has a cluttered garage, and almost a 100-percent guarantee that she has a junk drawer somewhere in her home. If she always looks put together and polished, there are days when she struggles with her reflection in the mirror. While her kids may always look joyful and happy, there are moments of tears and meltdowns. It's just that you don't see these messier moments on camera, or don't witness them in the fifteen seconds that you see her at Target. But she's a human being, remember? She has her messy moments, just like each of us.

I don't write that to give you permission to relish in her messiness or to rejoice over her struggles. I simply want to remind you that she's human. And while her humanity means she has rough days, it also means she's a beloved daughter of the Father. Sometimes we just need to remember that the person we're comparing ourselves to isn't some two-dimensional personality who crops up on our social media feed every once in a while.

If you're struggling to stop comparison in its tracks, spend some time getting to know the woman you're comparing yourself to. When you get to know her, you'll more than likely realize that she's a woman with gifts, talents, crosses, and experiences. You'll be able to recognize her whole story, not just the highlights of her Instagram story.

If your battle with comparison happens with the women in your small group, your coworkers, or your family, remember that those women have stories, too. But it's hard to conquer competition with celebration when the only story about her that you know is the one that you're telling yourself as you spiral into competition — that she has it all together, that she doesn't have places she's growing in her own life, and that she's a human being. Her true story is hard to see when you're busy comparing yourself to her, or trying to get one up on her in a spirit of competition and proving yourself.

So, make it a point to get to know her. Invite a woman in your small group to Mass and then grab coffee afterward. Sit down across the table from your coworker at lunch and ask her how her weekend was. The next time you're spending time with family, have an intentional conversation with your sister about her life and what's new — and really listen. Sitting down with the woman you compare yourself to on social media may not be an option. If the miles separate you, though, it's still possible to kick comparison and competition to the curb. One way that I've found that is truly guaranteed to work, regardless of how many miles separate you and the woman you're comparing yourself to, is to spend time in prayer.

It's not that prayer will change the situation you find yourself in. Her life, kids, wardrobe, career, talents, taste in home décor, and successes will still be the same. The one thing that prayer does change is your heart, though. As you bring this woman before the Lord and ask for the grace to see her as he sees her, your heart starts to soften. Gradually, with the Lords' grace, you'll start to see her through his eyes. If you're comparing yourself to a woman you've never met but follow on social media, make it a point to pray for her by name — her real name, not her Instagram handle. Remind yourself in prayer of her humanity, of her story. And ask the Lord for the grace to love her as his beloved daughter and your sister in Christ.

Are You Setting Yourself Up for Failure?

Does a scroll through your Instagram feed fill you with feelings of dread, competition, and negativity? First, like all things, start by examining your own heart for friendship (flip back to chapter one for an in-depth walk through that process). But after you've examined your own heart and you're still struggling, it might be time to take a closer look at the accounts that fill your feed.

"Imagine if you walked into a room and saw all the people you follow on social media, who would you excitedly rush up and greet? Who would you hug, chat, and laugh with? More importantly, who would you avoid like the plague? Just thinking about that very scene in your mind will help you nail the ones who don't need to be part of your social media friendship quilt," writes Flic Taylor. "Your social media moments should consist of you commenting, liking, sharing and smiling. The warning signs of those who need to hit the bucket are the one which causes your silences, sneers, sighs and self-doubt."[3]

The beauty of Instagram is that you can curate a feed that fills you, instead of a feed that tempts you into comparison and jealousy. It's okay to take a break from following accounts that are particular jealousy or comparison triggers for you. Clicking "unfollow" doesn't mean that you think this person doesn't have dignity, or doesn't deserve to be seen. Instead, that choice recognizes where you are and how you interact with her content.

Unfollowing someone on social media isn't a permanent decision, either. If you need to take some time and space to heal the wounds at the root of your tendency to compare, you can always follow her again after you've found healing. And just because you unfollow someone for a season on social media, it doesn't mean you can't pray for her, or be her friend. In fact, it could be just the reset you need to truly encounter this woman as a friend off-screen and get to know her true story.

Are You Ignoring the Good Because of the Should?

Have you caught yourself thinking that the gifts and talents that God gave you aren't enough, and they should look like something different instead? Something more like what someone else has? Have you rearranged your house after seeing a picture of a perfectly curated living room in your Instagram feed? Have you tossed out clothes that you genuinely like because they don't look like what other women are wearing to Mass at your parish?

If you answered "yes" to any of those questions, grab a pen and piece of paper or open up the notes section on your phone. Let's take some intentional time to recognize the real gifts, blessings, and joys God has given *you* specifically in your life. In a homily recently, my parish priest said that we do a great job at exercising our imagination — we think of what we want, what our life could be like if only God gives us something we think we're missing. But he encouraged us to exercise our memory, and intentionally recall the times that the Lord has already blessed us, which we often forget. So first, start by thinking about your greatest joy right now. It could be your marriage, a great friendship, an insight you had in prayer recently. Then, write that joy down and thank God in prayer for it — this doesn't have to be an elaborate or long prayer, just a short thank you to the Lord for his generosity.

Now, think of times in your life where you've felt the most alive, when you were incredibly aware of God's presence in your life. Maybe it was when you started the first day at a job that you love, or when you discovered a creative talent that you love spending time doing. Perhaps what comes to mind is how it felt to climb a mountain peak or feel so small under a starry night sky in the country. Or perhaps it was a moment in relationship with someone you love, like when your spouse proposed or a deep, heart-to-heart conversation with a dear friend. Thank God for those moments, those experiences where you were assured of his presence and his goodness.

Finally, think of times that you've felt comfortable and confident doing something. Are you a fantastic organizer who thrives in creating custom excel spreadsheets? Or maybe you have no problem sharing the story of your faith, confidently telling others how God has impacted and changed your life. Perhaps you're an extrovert who comes alive greeting people you don't know and introducing them to others, creating and building community. Name those areas of confidence and thank the Lord for those talents and the ways you've been able to use them to build up his kingdom.

All of these things on the list that you've just written down are gifts from the Lord. He loves you and calls you good — and he's also calling you to grow closer to him through gratitude for those gifts. "We have to first learn to see how, what the Psalmist calls the 'desires of the heart', your loves and passions, your family and career, your hobbies, and intimate companions along the way, have all been the ways God intends to get your attention and win over your trust," explains Father David Vincent Meconi, S.J.[4]

I don't know your story or the specific things that come to mind when you think of your joys, talents, and treasures. But I do know without a shadow of a doubt that God has blessed you. He's given you the gift of life itself, after all. And when we get caught up in comparing our experience to everyone around us, it's easy to lose sight of the specific ways that the Lord is romancing our hearts, showing us that he is a trustworthy Father.

Taking time to recognize the gifts and talents that God has blessed you with isn't prideful or boastful. Instead, it's an act of praise, recognizing the goodness of the Lord and the ways that he's blessed you. If comparison is something you struggle with regularly, add space in your daily prayer time to practice gratitude for the gifts that you recognized that day from him, big or small. Practicing gratitude daily not only helps you become more aware of the many reasons you have to thank God; it also helps you recognize the gifts of others as just that — gifts, not opportunities to compare or compete.

When we ignore the good and beautiful gifts from the Lord in our own lives because we're caught up in comparison, we're falling prey to what Dr. Meg Jay calls the "tyranny of the should."

"Shoulds can masquerade as high standards or lofty goals, but they are not the same. Goals direct us from the inside, but shoulds are paralyzing judgments from the outside. Goals feel like authentic dreams while shoulds feel like oppressive obligations. Shoulds set up a false dichotomy between either meeting an ideal or being a failure, between perfection and settling. The tyranny of the should even pits us against our own best interests," writes Dr. Jay, a clinical psychologist who specializes in adult development.[5]

The next time you're tempted to change something (an outfit, a meal plan, a couch placement in your front room) because it doesn't look like what you think it should, take time to discern the reasons behind the "should." Then, take those insecurities and perceived judgments to the Father and ask him to speak His truth over them.

Every time I've done this, he's reminded me that my value to him isn't found in the size of the clothes in my closet, the number of followers I have on social media, or the daily logistics of my prayer life. My preciousness rests in the fact that I'm his beloved daughter, who he's created and called good.

And he calls you good, too, sister. Not good in comparison to the woman beside you. Simply good in his eyes, no comparison needed.

Your story is not her story — thank goodness. If we all had the exact same experience of success, the same story when it came to living out the feminine genius in our daily lives as Catholic women, life would honestly be boring. There's an incredible diversity among our stories as women striving for the heart of the Father — and that's something to celebrate.

Are You Ready to Throw a Party?
Rejecting comparison and competition in favor of celebration might feel unnatural at first. You may feel like you're being fake. After all, celebrating the women in your life doesn't mean that you'll never struggle with comparison or competition again. Instead, celebration gives you a response you can turn to in moments

where you're tempted to compare yourself to the women in your life, on screen and off. Remember that authentic, Christ-centered, Eucharistic friendship with the women in your life is something that you can grow in. You can always become better at receiving and giving the gift (and genius!) of friendship. And creating a culture of celebration with those women is also something you can grow in and become better and better at over time.

Too often, we let fear and feelings hold us back from action. Because we still feel a little jealous, we might want to wait until we feel a little bit more celebratory before leaning into this kind of rejoicing with friends. But studies show that making changes in your behavior can transform the way you feel or think about a situation.[6] When you focus on acting in simple and intentional ways (like expressing gratitude or practicing kindness), your happiness does increase over time. In other words, it's okay to fake it 'til you make it in this situation.

What do these celebration parties look like practically? Okay, so maybe there's not actual confetti involved. In fact, the woman you're choosing to celebrate instead of compare yourself to might not even know that you're throwing a party in her honor. When you catch yourself comparing yourself to her, start small and simply thank God for the specific talent or blessing you're noticing in her life.

Maybe you find yourself struggling with comparison the most while you're browsing social media. When you see that old college friend who got the promotion you'd love to have or a baby you wish was in your arms, instead of just scrolling by and seething, leave a "congratulations" comment on the post that's making you a little green with envy.

And if conversations with friends off-screen are where you struggle the most, be intentional in the way you appreciate your friends' talents and gifts. When the conversation turns to the success a friend is experiencing, don't change the topic or dismiss her joy. Instead, ask her some intentional questions. Resist the urge to turn the conversation back to you and truly focus on her joy, blessing, or talent. And as hard as it can be, stay present in that conversation with her. Don't allow yourself to check out and start mentally measuring yourself up to her experience.

The first celebration party that you throw for a woman that you're comparing yourself to might seem forced. But that doesn't mean you should abandon the idea. You just need to grow in the art of hosting a good party to celebrate the accomplishments, gifts, and talents of the women around you. And how do you learn? You keep hosting parties. Over and over until, eventually, celebration becomes your default response instead of comparison or competition.

So let's start practicing the party-throwing. I'm right here alongside you, stumbling and sometimes throwing some parties that fall flat or turn into mental pity parties despite my best efforts. But perseverance in this mission to conquer comparison is worth it. Pass me a handful of confetti, let's get this celebration started!

Receiving the Gift of Celebration

The next time a friend compliments you on a gift or talent she recognizes in your story, accept the compliment and thank her instead of pushing the compliment away.

Giving the Gift of Celebration

The next time a friend shares exciting news or an important life update with you, whether it's over coffee or on social media, take time to intentionally enter into celebration with her — and thank her for the chance to join in the confetti-throwing!

Real Talk < *with* **Amanda Weeder**

Friendships That Welcome You In

The dishes are piled high, my toddler has just used my eyeliner to create what I am assuming is a great work of art — in his eyes — on my wall. Piles of laundry lay on my bed waiting for someone to fold. I shut my bedroom door, thinking maybe if I can't see all the messes, I will feel better (and the mess will magically disappear!)

My phone starts to buzz. I answer it and it's my husband. He's invited some good friends of ours over for dinner, sending me into complete panic mode. "What do you mean? We can't have people over tonight. I don't feel like it and besides, this house is a mess! What will we eat? We have nothing! Tell them you didn't realize that tonight was not a good night and let's plan it for next week. Maybe."

Does this story sound familiar?

I've had many experiences of feeling like my home was not ready to have anyone over. Thanks to Pinterest, I had it in my mind that in order to have people over I needed some beautiful tablescape, along with delicious food that is cleverly placed on the plate and possibly some kind of theme or special occasion to have someone over. My home needed to be spotless in order to break bread with friends. When all of the stars align and all is well in the world, then I will finally be ready to invite people into my home.

Sounds super authentic and hospitable right? I hope you all speak fluent sarcasm.

The Bible speaks on hospitality many times, and not once does it mention needing to have a perfect home in order to invite others over. As it would turn out, showing others authentic hospitality doesn't even really have anything to do with your fancy table, your perfectly prepared food, or even a clean house. Instead, hospitality is a gift you give others and a way of life.

I once read somewhere that, "hospitality is love in action." The First Letter of John says, "Little children, let us not love in word or speech but in deed and in truth" (3:18). Taking action means we have to do something. We have to change our way of thinking on what hospitality actually means in order to be able to give this gift to others.

Not long after I tried to convince my husband why we couldn't possibly let people into our home, a friend came into my life who beautifully took action and showed me what true hospitality is. I was in a season of my life where I was searching for friends. As a relatively new mom, trying to find mom friends was proving to be difficult and downright annoying at times. But this particular friend stood out among the many women I had met before. At first, I couldn't quite put my finger on why I gravitated toward her. But reflecting on our story, I realize that it was her gift of hospitality was an incredible blessing in my own life.

I've always been a bit of a planner and a self-proclaimed home-body. This new friend of mine would spontaneously send a text, "Hey! What are you doing today? Playdate?" The planner in me would panic because I hadn't necessarily carved out time in my day for this, but I'd always respond, "Yeah! Sounds good!" and go to her house. Thank God I did.

I walked into her house and I felt immediately welcome. There were no set plans, her house wasn't always perfectly picked up, and lunch was usually a peanut butter and jelly sandwich with a side of Goldfish. Nothing fancy. Nothing super special. Yet everything was extremely meaningful to me. Among the chaos and noise that came with these playdates over the years, my heart began to understand what authentic hospitality looked like.

The gift of hospitality was a friend who confidently opened up her home to me no matter what the inside of the house looked like. She sat and listened to my parenting worries and anxieties while we passed pretzels to our toddlers to keep them distracted. Truly, these interactions within the four walls of her home changed my heart without me even realizing it.

Today, almost a decade later, our families are still close. I still get those spontaneous text messages inviting my family and me to come over for dinner. I love those text messages. They're a reminder that without being willing to give the gift of hospitality, you can easily miss out on so much in life.

If my friend had waited for the perfect moment to invite me over, we might never have had the opportunity to grow our friendship into what it is today. If I wait until my house looks Pinterest-worthy, then nobody will ever enter my home, and what a shame that would be. Perfection would keep me from the opportunity to love and serve others.

You know women who are lonely, women who need your gift of hospitality in their lives. So go ahead, sister, with your dishes piled high and laundry all over the bed. Open up your home, which is an extension of who you are.

I'll let you in on a little secret — people aren't really there to see how amazing your home is. They're there for you. They are there seeking that authentic friendship and community that their hearts so deeply desire.

Amanda Weeder is a wife and mom to four kids living in the heart of the Midwest. When she isn't chasing her littles around and picking up Legos, you can find her helping women from all over decorating their homes. Helping women tell their home's story and finding the dignity of home is a passion of Amanda's. She believes firmly that creating beauty within our homes is worthy and will most certainly lead to a more beautiful life internally as well as externally!

6

Opening Your Heart and Home to Friendship

On a warm summer morning a few years ago, I nervously climbed into my car and secured a casserole dish of warm cinnamon rolls in the passenger seat. I pulled out of my garage and made my way to a Blessed Is She women's brunch just a few minutes' drive from my house. The event was hosted by a woman I'd never met, and with one exception I'd never met any of the other women who were attending. In other words, it was a huge step out of my introverted comfort zone.

After I parked my car and made my way up to the front door, I nearly chickened out. Wouldn't it be easier to just turn around, go home, and eat all of these cinnamon rolls by myself? Maybe. But I rang the doorbell anyway. Jill, the hostess, answered the door and asked for my name so she could make a nametag for me. Then she swept me into the kitchen to make me a cup of coffee, which she poured into a little vintage mug that she mentioned looked like my style. She also introduced me to the other guests who were spread out from her kitchen to her living room.

Throughout the morning, I saw Jill do this over and over — stop whatever she was doing, go to the door and greet the women who were slowly pouring into her front room. She encountered each and every one of us with a spirit of true receptivity — looking each of us in the eye, repeating our names and then introducing us by name to new friends, and making sure everyone had something to drink and eat before settling in on comfy couches and folding chairs. Everyone had a spot to sit. Everyone had a mug of coffee. Everyone was known, seen, and loved.

As the morning continued, Jill led a conversation on the beauty of prayer. She invited each woman to share what was working for her in her current season of life, and asked intentional follow-up questions that helped everyone there get to know the woman who was sharing her story even better. Whether someone had just a few sentences to add to the conversation or a lengthy response, each one was heard. As women shared and dove into further conversation, Jill gathered plates, refilled coffee mugs, and held babies so moms could get a chance to eat with both hands.

At the end of the morning, Jill led a prayer to close our time together and then sent us home with a small gift — a little wine charm with a small saint medal attached to it. She'd crafted and prayed over each parting gift and encouraged women to pick their favorite saint out of the selection or get to know a new-to-them saint. As we gradually started heading out the door and back to our cars, Jill thanked everyone for coming and made sure everyone had their casserole dish in hand and knew that she was so glad we were able to make it.

Every time I see a small vintage coffee mug at a thrift store or in a coffee shop, I'm reminded of Jill's mastery of the art and genius of friendship and hospitality. When I host friends for dinner or brunch, I often think back to the way that Jill paused whatever she was doing to greet a guest at the door, and the interest in her eyes that shone when you shared something new about yourself.

My prayer is that as you're reading this, you're thinking of your own Jill — a woman in your life who lives hospitality beautifully, in a way that honors the stories of those she invites into her house. I'm always in awe of these women's incredible gift.

I remember leaving that brunch inspired by Jill to live hospitality in my own life, and being inspired to start inviting more friends into my home. Up until that point, I thought hospitality in my small one-bedroom apartment was impossible. But Jill's hospitality showed me that I was thinking about hospitality all wrong.

God Created Our Souls for Hospitality

Too often when we think of the phrase "hospitality," we picture a Joanna Gaines-inspired home with a sparkling, impeccable hostess dressed in a pair of white jean capris and cute wedges, ready to pour perfectly crafted mimosas while standing on her beautifully decorated front porch. The danger of that commercialized, HGTV idea of hospitality is that it tempts me to believe the lie that since I don't have a shred of shiplap in my home, and I select wine based on the picture on the label, that I am obviously going to be a total hospitality failure.

But as Catholic women, hospitality isn't something just for those of us who have an open concept kitchen or the talent of putting together a charcuterie board. Just like the feminine genius and female friendship is for every woman, the Lord invites each and every one of us to grow in the virtue of hospitality. And if we need even more convincing, Christ tells us that he will judge us by our ability to love and welcome others at the end of time. In other words, hospitality isn't optional. It's inherent to our lives as Christians.

In the Gospel of Matthew, Christ describes the final Judgment to his followers. "Then the King will say to those at his right hand, 'Come, O blessed of my Father, inherit the kingdom prepared for you from the foundation of the world; for I was hungry and you gave me food, I was thirsty and you gave me drink, I was a stranger and you welcomed me, I was naked and you clothed me, I was sick and you visited me, I was in prison and you came to me'" (Mt 25:34–36). For those gathered at the end of the world who were unwilling to see the face of Christ in the hungry, thirsty, lonely, or weighed down by burdens, eternal punishment awaits.

But the last Judgment isn't the only place we see hospitality emphasized in Scripture. Jesus often sits down for a meal to encounter others, like when he went to Zacchaeus' house after meeting him on the road. He works his first public miracle at a wedding party. Mary bathes the Lord's feet with oil while he's reclining for dinner. We also find Christ establishing the Sacraments of Reconciliation and the Eucharist around the dinner table at the Last Supper.

All throughout his time here on earth, since the "Son of Man has nowhere to lay his head" (Mt 8:20), Jesus relied on others to open up their homes to him so he could have a place to rest during his time of ministry. Today, he invites us to open up our very hearts and bodies to encounter him. When we grow in the art and genius of hospitality as we invite Christ into our lives, we recognize that he is both guest *and* host; in fact, that's what we call the Eucharist — the host. As we welcome him into our bodies and receive him in the Eucharist, we can ask him for the grace to transform our hearts and our lives, to live his life within us. It's only when we're filled with Eucharistic grace that we're able to strive for Eucharistic friendships in our daily lives — we truly become what we eat.

Although this call to hospitality is for every Christian, man or woman, women have an innate ability to recognize Christ in the faces around them. We've already talked about what St. Teresa Benedicta of the Cross, sometimes better known as Edith Stein, wrote about how God created the souls of women when she explained that, "The woman's soul is fashioned as a shelter in which other souls may unfold."[1] But that specific quote is worth revisiting within the context of hospitality. Our very souls are places where others can come to simply exist, to be authentic and vulnerable. Note that Saint Teresa doesn't talk about a perfectly decorated home or curated playlist as requirements for places where others can unfold. Only our souls are needed, because inherently, the feminine soul is a place where hospitality can thrive.

It's okay if your house is messy. And — an even more freeing truth — you don't need to clear all the dirty dishes from your sink or shove your unfolded laundry pile in the closet in order to invite others in. It's okay if your heart is messy, too. You don't have to have it all together before you open the door of your home to others, or before you open the door of your heart, either.

Jill's home wasn't immaculate or perfect. Instead, it was beautiful and cozy, a reality that was amplified by her warm laughter and kindness. Her soul was a place where women could unfold — and her home was simply a mirror image of that.

The Genius and Gift of the Invitation

Hospitality can thrive in many places — from our homes to grocery store parking lots, from conversations and phone calls to direct messages on Instagram. But regardless of where we're creating places for others to unfold, have the entirety of their story be seen, and simply exist as children of God, the one thing that always comes first is an invitation — an invitation to grow deeper in friendship. And given that we're more lonely than ever as a society, that is an incredibly valuable invitation to extend to the women in our lives.[2]

"Perhaps that's one of the greatest contributions we can each make to form a culture that's more lovely than coarse: to cultivate the gift of being able to bring women together," writes Margaret

Brady. "Even though I don't think that's my main calling, I want to make room for it within my personal mission. I want to keep an eye out for women who are lost and lonely and be courageous enough to connect them with women who will know how to welcome them in."[3]

You don't need to create the perfect space to welcome others and make room for them in your home, in your heart, and in your story. You don't need to be a great cook, or the perfect conversationalist. In fact, the more that you aim for perfection when it comes to welcoming others, the more hospitality risks being transformed from a virtue into a performance. Perfectionism impairs your gift of feminine sensitivity — instead of noticing the needs of others and encountering them, you turn your focus inward and become overly concerned with how your practice of hospitality looks from the outside.

Hospitality isn't just about your ability to put together a good charcuterie board (although in a spirit of total honesty, I love a good Trader Joe's charcuterie spread). Hospitality lies in your ability to be sensitive to the women around you — aware of the room, aware of each person, and in your ability to create a place for women to unfold. When you're "performing" hospitality, you're drawing the attention toward yourself and your ability to set a good scene and make a good spread. When you're focused on the virtue of hospitality, you're directing your attention to the other — and that's when you're able to enter into giving and receiving the gift of friendship through hospitality.

When I think about biblical hospitality, the women who first come to mind are Mary and Martha. These two sisters hosted the Lord in their home, and you likely know their story well. Mary sits at the feet of Jesus, while Martha burdens herself with the to-do list of the day — cooking, serving, cleaning. Exasperated, she asks the Lord to remind Mary of the things that need to be done and to get up and help. Then Christ tells Martha that Mary has chosen "the better part," and points out that Martha isn't just busy with the to-do list; she's anxious and worried about it (see Lk 10:38–42).

Martha gets a bad rap in a lot of homilies and interpretations of this passage. Why wasn't she able to just drop it all and be with Jesus? Yet every time I read this Scripture, I see myself in Martha. Martha is doing things that are good (and hospitable!) when Christ enters her home. She's making food and serving Jesus and his apostles. The only problem is that she's forgotten something important — the presence of Christ just a few rooms away.

"In bustling about and busying herself, Martha risks forgetting — and this is the problem — the most important thing, which is the presence of the guest, Jesus in this case. She forgets about the presence of the guest," Pope Francis explained during an Angelus reflection in 2016. "A guest is not merely to be served, fed, looked after in every way. Most importantly he ought to be listened to. Remember this word: Listen! A guest should be welcomed as a person, with a story, his heart rich with feelings and thoughts, so that he may truly feel like he is among family. If you welcome a guest into your home but continue doing other things, letting him just sit there, both of you in silence, it is as if he were of stone: a guest of stone."[4]

The women that we invite into our hearts and homes aren't statues to arrange around the table to create the perfect dinner scene. They're not props in a Pinterest-worthy scape. They're daughters of God and they have a story to tell. And if you open your door (and your ears!) you will be given the incredible gift of friendship they're offering — if only you stop and encounter each one.

This is the kind of listening and encounter the pope and Christ are inviting us into. You can live this hospitality in intentional times carved out for friends, like hosting brunch or small group in your home. But it's also about leaving room in the margin of your day so that you can "waste" time with a friend. In today's world that values productivity and business, having the freedom to allow yourself to be interrupted and be present with someone is an invaluable gift. Instead of letting yourself be burdened with the "doing" part of serving, focus on being. Be present and listen without checking your email or refreshing your Facebook feed, and surrender even the schedule of your day to the Holy Spirit. You don't need to have all the answers to a friend's problems when she unexpectedly calls just needing someone to listen. You don't have to have the perfect responses. In fact, what you *don't* say may be the most important part of hospitality: your presence, rather than your words.

"Not much is necessary to welcome [Jesus]," Pope Francis continues. "Indeed, only one thing is needed: listen to him — this is the word: listen to him — be brotherly to him, let him realize he is among family and not in a temporary shelter." Is your soul a place where the women in your life can unfold? Is it a pop-up shop or something that lasts? Since we live in a transitory world, and one that sometimes feels as temporary as an Instagram story, the gift of your time and your steady presence is invaluable in true sisterhood.

The Virtue of Hospitality in Daily Life

Regardless of what season you're in or the square footage of your home, you can grow in the virtue of hospitality, starting today! Hospitality isn't a pie-in-the-sky abstract concept or a quote to embroider on a pillow, but rather a lived virtue that takes practice. So, before we close this chapter, I want to offer you a few tried-and-true pieces of practical hospitality advice.

First, remember to keep it simple. When you invite someone into your home or your heart, it's tempting to go *all out*. Believe me, I've been there. The very first women's night I hosted in our first apartment, I set out a fancy coffee bar, complete with every possible thing you could pour into a coffee mug. From honey to creamer, it was all set out — complete with adorable mugs and a freshly made carafe of steaming hot coffee. But it was a women's *night* small group. And despite the fact that the coffee spread was to die for, no one was quite down for drinking a cup and not falling asleep until two in the morning. I got so wrapped up in the appearance of everything that I forgot to consider even the time of day. If you're wondering, I was the only one who drank a cup of coffee, and yes, I was indeed awake through the wee hours of the night, deeply regretting that choice. The point of this story is this — keep things simple. You don't need an elegant spread or intricate theme. You don't have to redecorate your home to reflect the season of the year before you invite someone in. Your guests are coming to see you and get to know your story. Hosting can be as simple as throwing a plate of crackers and cheese out on the coffee table or having a bottle of wine on hand. But significantly more important than what you have to eat or drink, work to encounter the story of the women who come through your front door. If they leave listened to, respected, and seen, you could have a plate of Cheerios on the table and it wouldn't matter.

If the idea of opening your home up to others seems completely unattainable, start small. You could begin by hosting guests you know well. A movie night with your sister or a close friend is a lot less pressure than hosting women you just met, and gives you the chance to practice this art of hospitality with women you're already comfortable with.

Another way to take the pressure off is to always cook the same meal for new friends. I learned this tip from Kendra Adachi, who writes about the principle of "deciding once" in her book, *The Lazy Genius Way*. When I take one of the decisions of hospitality off the table by deciding that I'm always going to make the same meal when hosting someone for the first time, the invitation becomes easier. I've settled on cranberry chicken wraps — I can throw the chicken in the Instant Pot and be totally present with my guests while everything cooks without my constant attention. Maybe you have a dish you can make in your sleep; that's the one to make when you're hosting someone new. It takes some of the decision fatigue away from the invitation. And if your guests offer to bring something to complement the main meal, you'll already know what you're making and what gaps they can fill with their generous offer.

Don't be afraid to invite the women you're hosting to share in the preparation. Giving a guest something to do with her hands can help her feel more at home in your house, and spend time with you in a comfortable way. Whether that means setting the table or stirring the pot of soup on the stove, invite her into the process of hospitality. Not only does this create an opportunity where you can ask for help and be vulnerable with your guests, it also helps guests to give the gift of hospitality in some small way back to their host.

Host women in a way that honors your story and gifts. If you are fantastic at hosting, but are worried about the size of your apartment, host your friends for drinks before heading out to a local restaurant for dinner. If you love spending a Sunday afternoon leisurely resting and relaxing, invite friends over for an afternoon by the fire in the winter, or out on the back porch on a summer evening to simply exist and be part of your routine. Host in a way that invites women into your way of life — an event that would exist whether they were there or not, which gives you the space to be your most authentic self.

Finally, remember that hospitality is both an art and a virtue, which means you can grow in it! Although those first invitations might feel awkward and unnatural, the more that you invite a new or old friend into good conversation, the more natural hospitality will become for you. We learn hospitality by being hospitable. Whether you encounter a woman at a coffee shop after daily Mass or host a friend for her birthday party, don't be afraid of a situation that doesn't look like what you expected. The Lord takes the gifts and talents we bring to the table and multiplies them. Draw support from the perfect Host and the Blessed Mother and open up your heart and home to the women in your life.

Our Lady shows us the ideal, what to aim for in our hospitality, through her receptivity to the will of God. She gives her ultimate "yes," her fiat, at the Annunciation, setting aside her plans for her life and accepting the will of God. But that yes isn't just a one-time event. Her gift of total hospitality to the Lord echoes throughout her entire life. During the nine months of her pregnancy, her every encounter with those she met included bringing Christ physically to them. We don't know much about those hidden years of Christ's life in the little house at Nazareth. We don't have a Scriptural account of Mary's daily acts of hospitality with Joseph and Jesus. But her quiet faithfulness can remind us that hospitality is not just for the guests who come into our homes; it's also for the people who share our homes with us, day in and day out. Ironically, the people we love the most can be the people who we find the most challenging to offer service and hospitality to. But we can look to Our Lady as an example of what it means to serve them with generosity and love.

Our Lady's gift of hospitality is life-giving and life-changing. In fact, Mary's gift of noticing marks the beginning of Christ's public ministry. In Scripture, it's Our Lady who recognizes that the couple at the wedding at Cana has run out of wine, bringing the problem to Jesus and trusting he will take care of it (see Jn 2:3). When we first start hosting women, we can start by inviting Christ and Mary to be alongside us, hosting and serving others with us. But the more we grow in hospitality, we can take the next step of not only asking Jesus and Mary to be with us, but to be *in* us, to live their lives through us.[5] Then, as we open ourselves to encounter and listen to women in our lives, we can pray the prayer that Pope Francis prays, saying, "May the Virgin Mary, Mother of listening and of service and of attentive care, teach us to be welcoming and hospitable to our brothers and our sisters."

Receiving the Gift of Hospitality

When you're talking with a friend in person, whether it's at a coffee shop or at work, receive her story in a spirit of hospitality and sensitivity. Put down your phone, look her in the eye, and listen to receive, not respond.

Giving the Gift of Hospitality

The next time you see a woman at Mass who you don't recognize, make it a point to stop and say hello, introduce yourself, and learn her name. Then, the next time you see her, greet her by name. And don't be afraid to invite her to grab coffee or a meal after Mass. After all, there's no better combination than sacramentality and hospitality!

Real Talk *with* **Sarah Burns**

Friendships That Grow in Healthy Vulnerability

Regina and I looked at each other with tear-stained eyes in that Chick-fil-A parking lot, and we both knew that our friendship had transitioned into a deep and lasting place.

But back up. How did we get there? Not instantaneously and not overnight. This was far from our first lunch date together, and far from the first time we cried — or laughed — together, either.

Regina and I first met at work. Her first impression of me (power heels and makeup) was "fake" and my first impression of her (long flowing hair and dragon sketches) was "nerd." This does not sound like the beginning of a long and lasting friendship, but I think we both saw glimpses of what was underneath from the very beginning. Neither of us wanted to stay hidden. The gradual un-veiling — the process of vulnerability — became both the organic growth and firm foundation of our friendship.

We quickly discovered our mutual Catholicism and love of lit-erature. Through sharing faith and story, we began to get to know each other more deeply. We shared faith in a small group togeth-er and bonded with other women as well. Keeping our friendship open and nonexclusive enabled us to not become possessive of the other in friendship, and to get to know other sides of each other that we otherwise might not have seen.

I can't overstate the importance of growing in good humor together. Realizing that neither of us took ourselves too seriously — that we both could take a joke well — lent an ease to our rela-tionship from the start. Humor played a big part in developing our trust in each other as true friends and gave us the foundation of joy capable of bearing heavier moments.

We learned to encourage and challenge each other as we earned the right to speak into the other's life. We learned to apologize when we messed up, and to forgive. We learned how to argue and disagree passionately, while loving no less deeply — a trait so rare to find in friendship. We shared our triumphs and our failures. I learned to walk with and support her in her vocation of marriage, as she loyally supported me throughout my own journey of vocational discernment. As we learned that our friendship was a safe place for anything and everything that was going on in our lives, we learned to let each other into our hearts.

From all of this came that moment, sitting in a parking lot over a lunch break, when a deeper dam broke between us and the tears came. And because of that foundation, we were both prepared to give, and to receive, this precious gift of vulnerability in which we began to share our deeper wounds.

Love never forces. This is the characteristic most dear to me in my vulnerability with Regina, and hers with me: freedom.

Freedom provides the safe, loving garden in which true vulnerability can flourish. I have discovered in other failed friendships how forced vulnerability chokes out true friendship; my friendship with Regina has taught me much about growing together, season by season, and allowing vulnerability to unfold in time with grace and freedom.

Regina is a friend with whom I can entrust not just my humor and my hurts but also, more precious still, my joys. My joys are certainly more dear and more eternal than my sorrows! Sharing deeply of our joys and creativity has become the most important piece of our friendship, and the one we will bring with us to heaven.

Vulnerability in friendship has slowly worked on my heart, reminding me that while certainly we are strangers and sojourners on the earth, with true friends, we don't have to journey alone.

Sarah Burns is a Catholic woman who tries her best to live out the words of Saint Irenaeus that "the glory of God is a man fully alive." She has a background in art, music, literature, and ministry. Her love for mountains and books takes a back seat only to her love for Jesus and people. Often found on the trails on warm sunny days, and curled up with a book and a hot drink on the cold and rainy ones, she tries to follow Jesus wherever he leads.

7

Healthy Vulnerability in Friendships

As we've discussed, our desire for friendship can't be really satisfied with superficial conversations about the weather and our current Netflix favorites. Many, if not most of us, are tired of small talk and are ready for real, raw, healthy, and authentic connection and deeper conversation. But how in the world do we go deeper? We can't connect on a heart level with the women in our life without the gift of vulnerability. If you're anything like me, the concept of vulnerability is intriguing, slightly intimidating, and a little squirm-inducing, for multiple reasons.

Vulnerability is often understood as being open to the possibility of being hurt, either physically or emotionally. The word could call to mind an image like a chink in a suit of medieval armor, exposed to a devastating blow. I don't know about you, but at first glance that doesn't sound like something that I want much of in my daily life, or in my friendships with women. In fact, if I'm being totally honest, it sounds like something I'd like to avoid altogether.

Being vulnerable and receiving others' vulnerability absolutely includes the risk of being hurt. When you share with a friend something that you're struggling with, or even a part of your past that you're hesitant to bring to the light, you're revealing an intimate part of your story. When that is shared with someone trustworthy, it has the capacity to deepen a friendship. You're saying to other women "I trust you with this part of myself." But when those same things are shared with someone who isn't trustworthy, that information can be used maliciously. Revealing these parts of your story shows that chink in your armor. Trustworthy, authentic, and Eucharistic friends are able to see what you share with them as a gift, a way to get to know and love you in a deeper way. Women who can't be trusted with that part of your story are the ones who would see that weak point in your armor and use it to exploit or manipulate you.

Perhaps you know the pain of being wounded by a friend you trusted all too well. Or you might be terrified of being vulnerable only to find out that you shared that part of your story and your soul with the wrong person. Revealing parts of our heart in moments of vulnerability can be scary. But if we don't allow ourselves and our friends this gift, we'll always operate under a mask of everything being "fine." We'll never experience Eucharistic sisterhood without vulnerability. We won't be able to give or receive the gift of friendship without this leap into the deep end with the women in our lives who we trust.

When I first started diving into intentional sisterhood, I knew that vulnerability (whatever it was) had a role to play in that journey. But defining vulnerability and embracing it in my daily life seemed like an impossible and messy task.

So, like a typical type-A organizer, I sat down and started to research. My secret (or not so secret?) hope was that I could avoid it all, and stay comfortably safe, away from the challenge of vulnerability. But I couldn't have been further from the truth. As I went down rabbit hole after rabbit hole of articles, blogs, and podcasts on the subject, I ended up on YouTube, hoping someone would be able to unlock the mystery of vulnerability for me.

That's when I encountered Dr. Brené Brown, who has spent more than six years studying vulnerability and shame. Little did I know that when I sat down to watch her TED Talk, "The Power of Vulnerability," in my little one-bedroom apartment that her research and wisdom would drastically impact my life and my friendships. I know for a fact that I'm not the only one who has been impacted by Brown's presentation — there's a reason her video on YouTube now has fifty-two million views and counting after ten years.

Brown defines vulnerability as "uncertainty, risk, and emotional exposure." It's that feeling in the pit of your stomach when you take even the tiniest step outside of your circle of comfort or do something that means you're out of control of the situation. Vulnerability is texting the woman from your parish and asking her if she'd like to grab coffee sometime — that vulnerable friend ask that opens you up to the possibility of rejection. It's also vulnerable to share with a friend about a dream that the Lord is inviting you to pursue, or a ministry you think he might be calling you to. Vulnerability is telling a close and trustworthy friend that you're struggling with depression. Or vulnerability could be admitting that you need help taking care of yourself and asking a friend if she'd be open to checking in with you to make sure you're actually doing okay. If you're anything like me, any and all of those leaps of vulnerability are terrifying. But when it comes to our friendships and becoming the women the Lord created us to be, healthy vulnerability is a necessity. So, take a few deep breaths with me. We can do this.

If we truly want to enter into authentic, wholesome, and holy friendship with the women closest and dearest to our hearts, we have to let them see our hearts. St. Teresa Benedicta of the Cross writes in *Essays on Women*: "Everywhere the need exists for maternal sympathy and help, and thus we are able to recapitulate in the one-word motherliness that which we have developed as the characteristic value of woman. Only, the motherliness must be that which does not remain within the narrow circle of blood relations or of personal friends; but in accordance with the model of the Mother of Mercy, it must have its root in universal divine love for all who are there, belabored and burdened."

Motherhood reveals so much to us as women about the beauty and hard work of vulnerability. Think about the vulnerability and openness that exists when a mother births her child into the world. She's splayed open, totally exposed. There's nothing to hide behind. She's raw and real. And often, she's surrounded by a team of women who are rallying around her, encouraging the opening-up of her very body so that new life can come into the world. They're midwifing alongside her, acknowledging her fears, cheering her on in those final excruciating moments, and rejoicing with her when she finally meets her child, at last.

Each and every one of us as women, regardless of our vocation, is called to be a mother, to the action and sacred work of mothering. You might mother children in the four walls of your home, or you could be a maternal source of comfort for a friend. This spiritual motherhood is not a consolation prize, second in some way to physical motherhood. Instead, it's a freeing invitation to create, nurture, and love as only you can. This kind of mothering is in imitation of Our Lady's motherhood, which circles round and comforts each and every one of us as her children, pointing us back to the Lord.

We each possess an incredible feminine genius. The Lord created us to become places where other souls can unfold, where he can work in and through us to bring new life into the world. With our God-given gift of maternity and the help of grace we can create trustworthy, healthy places for women to encounter Christ in healthy vulnerability.

As Catholic women hungry for authentic friendship that finds its foundation in Christ, we need to dive deep into what vulnerability is and what it means practically for our lives. Perhaps the best way to do that is by examining what it *isn't,* an approach Dr. Brown takes in some of her presentations. Although this isn't an exhaustive list by any stretch of the imagination, here are a few things that vulnerability is not.

Vulnerability Is Not Weakness

Fear that others will see us as weak can hold us back from sharing intimately and vulnerably in our friendships. We might be worried that our petition for help leaves us open for someone to take advantage of us, to manipulate the very difficulty we trusted them with and use it against us.

We live in a culture that has embraced radical individualism, so much so that asking for help has become synonymous with weakness. It's easier to put on a mask of perfectionism, laugh, and say everything is fine, even when it's not. But when we shun the idea of asking for or accepting help, or give the impression we won't offer it when others need it, we're not able to truly enter into the giving and receiving of authentic friendship.

The first lie that the devil tells us as women — he started back in the Garden of Eden — is that vulnerability is for cowards. He encourages us to strike out on our own, to rely on no one — friends, family, even God — and to avoid pain. And that lie echoes throughout centuries of human history until we hear it in our hearts to this day as Catholic women. "Every ... woman has something in herself inherited from Eve, and she must search for the way from Eve to Mary," St. Teresa Benedicta of the Cross wrote. The devil desires to drill into our hearts the mantra that for things to go well, we have to take everything into our own hands and never relinquish control. Meanwhile, Our Lady offers us the perfect antidote in her fiat: "Be it done unto me according to thy will." She relies totally on the Lord and encourages us to do the same. Then, when we find our only source of security in the heart of God, we're able to recognize the women in our lives who can encounter our story, our vulnerability, with the Lord's compassion and mercy. This means that our vulnerability isn't a sign of weakness. In fact, it's incredibly courageous.

"What most of us fail to understand ... is that vulnerability is also the cradle of the emotions and experiences that we crave," says Dr. Brown. "Vulnerability is the birthplace of love, belonging, joy, courage, empathy, and creativity." Showing up and being truly present to the women in your life, flaws, imperfections, and all is scary. But when you open up and admit that you need accompaniment and encouragement, you not only are courageously being fully present as a daughter of God; you're also giving the women in your life an opportunity to receive your entire story and give you the gift of friendship in return.

"The beginning of love is the will to let those we love be perfectly themselves, the resolution not to twist them to fit our own image," writes Thomas Merton. "If in loving them we do not love what they are, but only their potential likeness to ourselves, then we do not love them: we only love the reflection of ourselves we find in them." Healthy (and courageous!) vulnerability opens up possibilities for us as women to embrace each other and the reality of our stories — stories that have joys, struggles, crosses, and celebrations all intertwined. Asking for help and revealing what you're experiencing isn't weakness. It's courageous. And it's the heart of friendship.

Vulnerability Is Not Easy

This is pretty much stating the obvious. If vulnerability takes courage and is not in fact a sign of weakness, it isn't going to come easily. That's true about both giving and receiving the gift of vulnerable authenticity. After all, vulnerability is one of the main things we desire our friends to give us, even while we can be incredibly hesitant to give it in return.

When we embrace vulnerability in pursuit of sisterhood, we teach each other how to receive the imperfect gift of ourselves and our stories. We aren't demanding that each of us show up perfectly put together, ready to be Wonder Woman. Instead, we're giving ourselves permission to need each other, and to acknowledge the fact that we aren't perfect this side of heaven. But vulnerability doesn't stop there. It also involves encouraging the women in our lives, and being encouraged by the women in our lives, to strive for wholeness and joy even in the challenging situations. Vulnerability is allowing women to journey alongside us in the midst of the hard season, rejecting the temptation to just chat about it after you've sorted through everything yourself. True vulnerability is opening up the door to your heart and letting the women you trust into the messy process and the in-between.

Again, not easy. But very much worth the challenge and struggle in order to come to a place in sisterhood where we're able to be truly ourselves and receive our friends' true selves.

Vulnerability Is Not Oversharing

Perhaps we've believed the myth that being vulnerable is all about sharing every detail of our stories with everyone, from our dear friends to random strangers on the internet. But being vulnerable in a healthy, wholesome way is not about oversharing. We're not participating in healthy vulnerability if we just spew our thoughts, emotions, and experiences out on an unsuspecting friend, or share about a situation with a total lack of prudence. So, if vulnerability isn't about oversharing, what is it all about?

Dr. Brené Brown suggests asking yourself a few questions to

discern whether you're sharing from a place of healthy vulnerability or not:[1]

1. Why am I sharing this?
2. What outcome am I hoping for?
3. What emotions am I experiencing?
4. What unmet needs might I be trying to meet?

Maybe you recently put in your two-weeks' notice at work. After disagreements with the way a situation was managed, you decided to look for a work environment that was more life-giving and better reflected your values. Now imagine that you sit down for lunch or coffee with a woman you used to work with at the company you quit. If you share about your frustrations with the company you used to work with, or even with a specific manager or mutual coworker, you might be hoping for some encouragement and affirmation of your experience. We all want to hear that we're right sometimes, right? You could be hoping for the outcome of some changes in the company culture, even though that might be something totally out of both you and your former coworker's control. Or you might even be wishing that your friend would throw in the towel too, just so the company would feel more repercussions. Your sharing could be coming from a place of heat-of-the-moment anger, or even a fear that your friendship with this woman might shift now that you won't pass by her desk every morning on the way to the coffee pot.

This isn't to say a good, long conversation about your situation with someone who knows that work environment you left is a bad thing. But if you're really in need of some quiet time alone to process your decision, or are operating out of a fear that you made the wrong decision, your vulnerability may step over the line into oversharing pretty quickly. Because you're not sharing from a place of healthy vulnerability, the conversation and experience you're sharing with your former coworker in this example isn't a gift for her to receive or for you to give. Instead, it's just oversharing and can actually harm your friendship.

It's also important to see what healthy vulnerability looks like in practice. Let's take the same situation we just processed in an unhealthy way and see what it would look like if shared from a place of authentic honesty. You sit down to coffee with the same coworker and maybe she asks how you're doing in your new job, or even asks you point-blank the reason that you left your old position. Maybe you still feel those same feelings — you're angry, worried about whether you did what you were supposed to do given the situation, and wonder if your friendship with your former coworker is on rocky ground because you don't share your day-to-day experience anymore.

When you take time to ask yourself the "why" behind your sharing, maybe you intentionally focus the conversation on your friendship. Instead of gossiping about the people you both knew at the office, you could share about your fear of your friendship with her shifting because you value the gift of her friendship and want to stay in touch. The outcome you're hoping for here could be resolving together to meet up for a happy hour or regular coffee to keep up to date on each other's lives. You might realize that the woman you used to work with is so much more than a coworker who you collaborated with on a project, and you don't want to lose her friendship simply because you don't work together.

When you take time to process through the questions Dr. Brown suggests, and realize what is healthy and what is unhealthy to share, the conversation shifts. You still are feeling the same feelings, but now you're navigating the conversation in a way that honors your story and the story of the woman sitting across the table from you. Vulnerability could also mean admitting that you're not quite sure what you're feeling about the situation yet because you haven't had time to really unpack it in prayer and silence. You could thank her for asking and ask if she'd check back in with you in a few weeks after you've settled into your new position and have had some time to think things through.

Healthy vulnerability isn't about how *much* you share with friends, but instead the *why* behind your desire to share. So, as you embark on this journey of embracing healthy vulnerability in your life and in your friendships, give yourself space to check your heart and your intentions as you enter into vulnerable conversations or situations with the women in your life.

Healthy vulnerability also means trying new things — even if you're worried that you'll look like a fool the first few times you try. Maybe that means getting out of your comfort zone and asking a friend to come over to your home for coffee, even though you're worried your house doesn't look exactly perfect. Healthy vulnerability means showing up for a friend who is in a season of suffering, even though you don't have all the answers and actually don't even know what to say — it's vulnerable to simply exist with them in that season without any answers and only your presence to offer.

Being vulnerable in a healthy way means honestly sharing what's on your heart, even if you're still processing how you feel or think about a certain subject, but allowing your friends into the messy grey middle of your discernment process.

Vulnerability Is Not a One-and-Done Experience

So, you shared your heart and your story in a vulnerable and courageous way with a friend who is close to you. Phew. Now you're done with vulnerability, right? Wrong. Friendship and vulnerability are both things that we can grow in, and that growth is never-ending and continuous. But the good news is that this continuous experience of vulnerability takes place in relationships where we are fully seen, known, and loved; relationships that are built on Christ.

These relationships aren't built overnight, though. Sure, you may have a connection with a woman in your life, but healthy vulnerability is not sharing the deepest desires and parts of your heart the first time you meet up for coffee.

Instead, vulnerability and trust are built up over little moments. It's a friend stopping what she's in the middle of when you share that you're really struggling after losing your dad. Or, it could be your friend swinging by to leave a bag of chocolate on your front porch after you share with her that you've had a really bad day at work. It might be noticing the way your friend didn't look you in the eyes when you asked how she was doing, and asking her if she's really okay. "In the richest friendships between women, there is an intimacy that differs from, and in some ways surpasses, that of other relationships," writes Margaret Brady. "The English word 'confidant' ultimately derives from the Latin verb *fidere*, which means 'to trust.' To have a confidant is to trust another person with your hardest truths, at moments of your greatest vulnerability; to trust that she'll rejoice in your victories and that she won't trample your spirit when it's broken, frightened, or ashamed."[2]

Vulnerability can seem an impossible mountain to climb. But creating an environment of healthy vulnerability in our friendships with women doesn't happen in one instance, with fireworks, a dramatic soundtrack, and all the emotions. Instead, it happens in those small moments where we turn toward each other as women and as sisters in Christ and let ourselves be truly seen by the women around us.

Vulnerability Is Not Avoidable

Still hoping to avoid vulnerability? Believe me, I get it. But vulnerability is unavoidable if we truly desire to enter into authentic feminine friendship. And if we try to avoid it, we're denying our friendships some incredible growth. Vulnerability allows us to go deeper in an intentional, healthy way with the women in our lives. It opens up our friendships to real conversations that touch on the deeper realties of our heart.

Are you ready to not only give but also receive the gift of healthy vulnerability? It's going to be challenging, and it's going to take courage. But it's also an incredible opportunity to enter into the friendship God calls us to as his daughters. After all, he sees our entire story — flaws and all — and is intimately aware of the ways that our hearts are hurting, and the ways we have hurt his heart through sin. Yet, despite all of this, he still desires an intimate relationship, a healthy friendship with us.

Vulnerability isn't weakness, and it isn't easy. It's not oversharing in a healthy or indulgent way, and it's not something we lean into during a conversation with a friend just one time in our lifetime. It's also not something we can avoid if we truly want to grow in a deeper, intentional, and healthy way with the women in our lives. Instead, vulnerability opens up our friendships to real conversations that touch on the deeper realties of our heart. The best example of healthy vulnerability we could possibly have is that of Christ, as he hangs on the cross and as he gives himself to us in the Eucharist. And if we're called to mirror that Eucharistic friendship in our friendship with the women in our lives, that means we have to stop avoiding vulnerability and instead, embrace it with open arms and open hearts.

Receiving the Gift of Vulnerability

The next time a friend shares, in a moment of healthy vulnerability, something challenging that she's going through, strive to be totally present to her. Listen as she processes and shares her experience and assure her that she's not alone.

Giving the Gift of Vulnerability

Has someone offered to help you with a particular struggle, but you've never taken them up on the offer, out of fear of taking advantage or inconveniencing them? The next time you need help, take a step towards healthy vulnerability and accept the help offered to you by a friend. Maybe that's saying "yes" to the offer of a meal train after the birth of your baby, or talking through a challenging situation with her. Trust your friends with your story, and trust that they're honest when they offer to journey alongside you in this season.

Real Talk *with* **Elizabeth Varga**

Friendships That Grow Online

During the summer of 2018, I had just started my blog, *The Plant-Based Catholic*, and I had only a few months' worth of recipes and posts on my site. My blog wasn't getting high traffic, so I was very surprised one day when I got an email from a girl named Lauren. She had found my website, and read about my desire to talk about the relationship between food and faith.

Unbeknownst to me, Lauren had been praying for the past few months, wrestling with this feeling of wanting to start a podcast. She was looking for a place to share her ideas as she grew in her Catholic Faith. In May, Lauren prayed a novena, asking the Lord for a sign that she should start a podcast. She very specifically asked to see a yellow rose for yes and a red rose for no. The last day of the novena was her brother's graduation from high school at which there were a plethora of both red and yellow roses. She was confused but was soon consoled by a friend who said that the Lord sometimes doesn't answer novenas. But in this situation, God didn't answer because Lauren already knew the answer: She wanted to start a podcast. She started writing and organizing for the podcast to launch at the end of summer.

In July, Lauren was scrolling through Instagram and came across my Plant-Based Catholic page. She saw my email and immediately contacted me. Lauren had always been interested in food and thought I would be an incredible interview for her podcast.

I was so excited! For a few weeks we bounced emails back and forth, learning more about each other and talking logistics of recording a podcast. I learned that Lauren's podcast was new, just like my blog. It was a great opportunity for both of us to grow our platforms, which had a shared audience.

As we conversed over email, Lauren told me that she was also a student at IU. She was from the area, but I lived a few hours away in Ohio. It was so crazy that we lived apart and randomly met through social media, but happened to go to the same school. As soon as we realized we could meet in person, we worked out the details to meet when I got back to campus in August.

When we first met in person it was a Friday. We sat together in a small, insulated room at the local library to record her podcast. She started asking me tons of questions about why I was vegan and the relationships that I saw between eating a plant-based diet and living a Catholic life. We talked about everything from the Eucharist as food, to the environment, to honoring God with our bodies.

Soon into the meeting, Lauren had forgotten the purpose of the interview. Conversation flowed so well — it felt like we had known each other for years, not minutes. After three hours we were forced to stop because we got kicked out of the room she had reserved.

Lauren spent some time after the interview listening to the recording and taking notes to figure out a story she could put together. She felt just like a journalist trying to crack a story. There was something more to what she was listening to that she couldn't quite put her finger on.

Luckily, we had agreed to meet again on Sunday to continue the conversation. When Sunday came, we sat again in the little room and our conversation picked back up right where it left off. We talked and talked. (As an introvert, this isn't something I do well, especially with strangers.) After several more hours, we were finished recording, but we knew that this was the beginning of something more.

The "something more" wasn't a story for a podcast, it was a desire for friendship. After the second interview we both wanted to meet up again. Lauren and I started meeting weekly because we knew we wanted to be in each other's lives.

The funniest part about our whole story is that Lauren's desire to start a podcast slowly went away as we became closer. We joke to this day that the only reason God wanted Lauren to start a podcast was so we could meet. The podcast never actually came to fruition, but our friendship bloomed.

We sat for long hours and talked about our lives, shared our testimonies, and walked side-by-side with each other in discipleship. We created accountability for each other as we walked through temptation, we went to Mass and adoration together, and kept each other on the straight and narrow. We've been best friends ever since.

Elizabeth Varga is the recipe developer and photographer behind the blog "The Plant-Based Catholic." She was born and raised in Cincinnati, Ohio, studied Economic Consulting and Business Analytics at Indiana University, and currently lives in Sandpoint, Idaho, working as the Content Marketing Specialist for Litehouse Inc. In her free time, when she's not cooking for her blog, Elizabeth enjoys drinking coffee, eating bananas, working out, listening to podcasts, and attending Mass. She is passionate about living a healthy lifestyle, sharing the message about how food and faith intertwine, and serving others through food.

8

Navigating the Digital World

In 2020, we watched the world as we knew it shut down around us. Grocery-store outings seemed like vacations from our home as we all sheltered in place thanks to COVID-19. Masks became the hottest accessory of the summer, literally. And as the world experienced a pandemic for the first time in our lifetime, we realized what a blessing friendship and community is, and how much we'd taken it for granted in the past. Many of us spent time on our friends' driveways, far enough apart to measure six feet but also close enough where we could see each other's faces and hear each other's voices for the first time in months. And let's not forget the fact that Zoom became a verb. Digitally attending baby showers, graduations, birthday parties, and weddings became the societal norm.

There's no denying that COVID threw a huge curveball at all

of us. But an unexpected grace from that season of masks, vaccines, and social distancing was that it provided me the space for some much-needed reflection on the beauty and challenges of digital friendship. Since all of my friendships went online at some point during that twilight zone of COVID, I realized that up until that point, I'd been categorizing my friendships with women into two buckets: my "real" friends and my "digital" friends. But if I learned anything from those days of toilet paper rushes and constant news-binging, it was the fact that digital friends can be real friends, and many of the women I connected with through social media became dear friends. During COVID, I spilled those two buckets. I quit thinking that the women I met online were somehow less my friends than the women I knew from my small group, church community, and local events. Those digital friendships weren't any more or less real. They just took intentionality, time, and commitment — like any friendship, on screen or off.

Even before COVID, our digital age means that the word *friend* is both a noun *and* a verb. This reality can be a huge blessing, especially if the off-screen opportunities for you to make new friends with the women in your life are few and far between — and don't worry, we're going to spend an entire chapter talking about how you can navigate this sticky season. But despite the convenience of having friends at a few taps of your thumbs on a touch screen, digital friendships can be a real challenge.

If you have an inkling that the quantity of your online friends doesn't automatically equate to quality of friendship, then you're right. In 2016, British anthropologist and psychologist Robin Dunbar conducted research on the quality of friendship that we have in our social, online networks.[1] His research revealed that out of the 150 friends the average Facebook user has, only fifteen of them could be counted as true friends, and only five of them would be called genuine friends. At first glance, Dunbar's research seems harrowing. If such a slim percentage of the women we know online can truly be counted as anything more than casual acquaintances, what's the point of even trying to log on to any app or platform in an attempt to make authentic connections? But don't look at those statistics and shrug off all digital friendships as fake. More than anything, I think Dunbar's statistics show that friendship online doesn't come with the click of a button. Instead, it takes time, commitment, authenticity, and healthy vulnerability to forge the bonds of friendship on social media and through apps.

I've encountered some incredible women on social media, especially through Instagram. There, my feed is filled with women who champion my good, call me to holiness, and correct me with kindness when I've misstepped. During the summer of 2020, I poured myself into those women. I couldn't get coffee in person with *anyone*. So instead, I took the opportunity to get to know the women who lived states, even countries, away. That summer we laughed together, cried together, grew together, and one woman who has since become a dear friend even swapped clothes with me. We shipped packages of clothing to each other across the United States for a cross-country fashion show of sorts.

Despite the bad rap that it gets, social media isn't the devil. I've met some close friends through social media. I've found amazing inspiration, incredible prayers, and indescribable community. But we do need to be conscious and clear with ourselves as we navigate any social media, and interact with it in a way that honors our true identity as beloved daughters of God, and that same identity in each woman we encounter online.

How to Be a Good (Digital) Friend

Just like we started this entire conversation together on friendship by examining our own heart, we should begin digital friendships by knowing our own heart, too — and I'm not talking about what heart emoji color you prefer to share when texting your friends. Remember, digital friendships *can be real friendships*. This means they deserve the same authenticity, healthy vulnerability, and honesty as any other friendship. So, while you're connecting with women online, don't give into the temptation to only talk about or show your digital good side. Sure, it's fun to share adorable pictures of your kids and the fun you had at the ladies' night at the local winery. But chances are, your children have at some point melted into a puddle on the floor of your local Walmart, and you may have recently hit a rough patch with the same friends you laughed with over a glass of chardonnay last weekend.

So, should you post the pictures of the meltdowns and over-share about your friendship woes? Not quite. When it comes to being yourself (and a better friend!) online, the key is to find the sweet spot of authenticity that stands in the middle of oversharing and selectively sharing. Being yourself online doesn't mean baring your entire story and soul to the internet — that's oversharing, and it's unhealthy for you and the women around you. "Oversharing is not vulnerability. In fact, it often results in disconnection, distrust, and disengagement," explains Dr. Brené Brown in her book *Daring Greatly: How the Courage to Be Vulnerable Transforms the Way We Live, Love, Parent, and Lead.*

So, what does sharing authentically online look like practical-ly? How can we find the middle between being yourself and over-sharing? It starts by examining your heart — notice a theme here? — and the reasons behind *why* you're posting something when you log onto your social media of choice.

Are you posting that selfie to celebrate something you're grate-ful for, and desiring the women in your life to rejoice alongside you? Girl, post that selfie. But if you're looking for the women in your life to compliment you because you think that will mean you are worthy and beautiful, it might be time to rethink before hit-ting "post." Even topics or thoughts that seem at first glance totally neutral or inherently good can be posted for the wrong reasons. For instance, if you're posting your thoughts about the spiritual book you're reading because you want everyone to think you have it all together and that you're virtuous and holy, you might want to spend time in prayer and ask the Lord to reveal why you have that desire.

Every post doesn't have to involve soul searching — there will be times where you simply want to share the joy of your cat settled on your laptop just because you think it's cute, or ask your online gardening community how to take care of an aloe vera plant your mom gave you for Christmas. The time to lean into this question and the way your heart reacts to it is when you're posting but you're not at peace. If you are paying attention, you'll get that little twinge that alerts you to the possibility that something is out of order. Then it's time to ask yourself if you're looking for something from friends that only Christ can give you. That's a good indicator to step away from the screen and into prayer, asking the Lord to be your only good, your only fulfillment like the psalmist says (Ps 16).

Remember, friendship is a gift both given and received. So, it's important to ponder why you're sharing something from the giving aspect of friendship, but also to consider what you're hoping to receive from the women in your life based on what you share as well.

"Some online friendships are built more on the 'projection' of how we would like to be seen by others — and not necessarily how we 'actually' appear in real life. We can be our 'best self' for virtual interactions in ways that it is difficult to maintain in real life," explains Dr. Suzanne Degges-White, a professor and chair of the Counseling and Higher Education department at Northern Illinois University.[2] That's the beauty of the giving side of friendship — presenting your whole, authentic self to another woman, rather than some more appealing and attractive version of yourself.

When you're able to approach digital friendships from a whole and healthy place, you can start new friendships (and rekindle old ones!) confident in the fact that you're sharing who you really are.

Connecting with New Friends Online

The internet, social media, and a host of different apps provide perfect places to form incredible and authentic feminine friendships. You can connect with women who live hundreds of miles away, on a different continent, or even the women in your own community who you might not have met otherwise. While there's no set roadmap for starting and developing an online friendship, there are a few places you can begin.

What articles do you love sending your friends? What subjects always come up when you hang out with girlfriends for coffee? Jot down a quick list of topics that are near and dear to your heart. Then, crack open your laptop (or unlock your phone) and look for ways to connect over those topics. Maybe you love books and are always sharing what you read last weekend. Check out your local library website to see if they're hosting any book clubs, digital or in-person. Perhaps supporting small businesses really lights you up. Browse the web and subscribe to some blogs or accounts of people who share your passion, and start a conversation by asking about their favorite small business. The possibilities for connection are endless, so starting with shared passions is a great way to intentionally connect.

Next, think about where you already like to spend time online. Maybe you love Instagram — make it a point to send a message to someone who you love following, but have never connected with beyond liking or commenting on her posts. Making a digital friend ask can be a little scary, but people love connecting over shared interests and loves. Let this woman know why you like following her account and ask her one intentional question as a conversation starter. You never know, that connection could lead to a great conversation and an even better friendship.

Don't forget the digital spaces that sometimes get dwarfed in comparison to the giants of social media like Instagram and Facebook. If you want to utilize the internet to meet local friends, check out sites like Nextdoor, which can connect you to your neighbors down the block. Another group that has helped me make some amazing friends is my local Buy Nothing group, which is based on giving generously to your neighbors.

Finally, the online resources available for Catholic women are endless. Whether it's connecting in a Blessed is She regional Facebook group or getting to know women around discussing a podcast or book, there is something out there for everyone. There are Facebook groups for Catholic women in any season of motherhood (like Catholic Mothers), Catholic mothers who are working full-time, part-time, inside or outside the home (Catholic Working Mothers), and women who love sharing their faith digitally (Catholic Women Bloggers). If you spend time on Instagram, accounts like theYoungCatholicWoman and Brick House in the City do a beautiful job representing the depth and breadth of the experience of living life as a Catholic woman today. Meanwhile, accounts like Catholic Women in Business create a digital space for women to grow professionally and spiritually — together. And if you're looking for a digital community without touching social media, you'll love the Blessed is She community platform, where you can ask other women for advice, prayers, or just have good conversation. Finally, online magazines offer a beautiful place to receive formation — and you can even meet fellow readers in the comment sections. If that's more your speed, check out websites like Verily, Radiant, or Theology of Home.

When you find a place online that inspires you and allows you to be your most authentic self, start investing some time into getting to know the women there. Share stories, send private messages, and be yourself. It's totally possible to carve out a space online where you can give and receive the gift of feminine friendship digitally.

Connecting with Friends from Past Seasons

Jeffrey Hall, a researcher from the University of Kansas, discovered that you need to invest somewhere between eighty and one hundred hours to become friends with someone.[3] And if you want to consider yourself close friends with someone, then you need to at least hit the two-hundred-hour mark together. That higher number can seem intimidating. After all, two hundred hours is more than a week straight. If your schedule is anything like mine, the idea of finding two hundred hours in your schedule can sound impossible. That's a lot of coffee dates. But don't despair! If starting from scratch and making new friends online seems overwhelming, try reconnecting. Chances are, you've probably already put in quite a few hours with women you loved spending time with, and life events and different seasons pulled you apart. This is where the beauty of social media really shines.

In college, I worked at a local bank and grew in friendship with quite a few of my coworkers. One woman in particular, Kayla, and I spent hours together on Saturday mornings, cashing checks and bonding over our shared love of gardens, books, and honest conversation. After I moved onto a job at my university library, Kayla and I lost touch for a while. Although I loved my job working the help desk and assisting my fellow college students with their research reports, I missed conversations with Kayla and those early Saturday morning hours in the teller window, sharing cups of coffee and laughter over a news story we'd both heard on the commute. A long time after college and years into my marriage, Kayla and I finally crossed paths again on Instagram. Now we're able to connect and chat about my daughters, Kayla's gardening adventures, and current events. Back at the bank, we easily hit that 200-hour mark of time spent together. Once we found each other on social media, it was easy to reconnect and invest in our friendship, despite our geographical and age differences.

Make an intentional decision to reconnect with an old friend from college or a former coworker and ask her how she's been since you last talked. Online platforms make it more than possible to revive friendships which would have normally been lost to time.

Giving and Receiving the Gift of Authentic, Digital Friendships

During college, I spent time on and off dating apps before I met Joseph, my husband. Curled up on my couch with a mug of coffee, I'd carefully create a dating profile that accurately displayed my likes, dislikes, hopes, and dreams. Then I'd work to connect with people who shared my interests, and struck up intentional conversations with them through meaningful questions. If you're working on growing in your intentionality with the women you know online, this probably sounds very familiar. The older that I get, the more I realize the uncanny similarities between online dating and developing digital friendships. The main difference, as a dear friend of mine once pointed out, is that I don't change outfits twelve times before connecting with online friends — which is honestly a relief.

Michelle Kennedy picked up on this reality too. She created a matchmaking app called Peanut for new moms, with the belief that helping moms connect would help eliminate the isolation that motherhood sometimes brings. "I founded Peanut because I became a mum and looked at the products around me and really felt like they didn't fit modern motherhood. I found it frustrating that there hadn't been any innovation for nearly twenty years," she explained in an interview with Forbes Magazine. "On a personal note, I found that moment of trying to find support and community difficult and challenging and I needed a tool like this, and the more women I spoke to the more I realized they felt the same. This is also with the backdrop of my day job at the time, and it felt somewhat obvious to take what I knew about dating and apply it to friendship."[4] Since over 500,000 women have downloaded the Peanut app, Kennedy knows she isn't the only one to desire a connection with other women living in the same season.

When I spent some time on online dating apps before meeting

my husband, it was tempting to just get to know someone casually in the messaging section, never taking things to an in-person chat or even a phone call. But I've found that temptation still exists, even though I deleted my dating apps. In a world that emphasizes the digital, it can be easy to let friendships languish in comment sections and direct messages. If we really want them to grow, we have to take those online friendships offline. I started using dating apps differently when I thought of them as a tool to meet people instead of dating people. Meeting people happened in the apps, but I had to be IRL for actual dates and relationships to form. I think we need to take a similar approach to the way we interact with the women we meet online. These digital friendships have the capacity to blossom into something so much more, but in order to discover the possibilities, we have to take those relationships offline.

Now, I'm not saying that this means you should pack your bags, buy a plane ticket, and go on a girl's weekend to meet your BFF from Instagram who lives in Boise and bonded with you over your mutual love for potatoes and praying the Memorare. Although I will say that the times I've been blessed to meet up in person with a digital friend, I've been able get to know her so much better and more intimately than I ever did in a chat box. If you ever do get the chance to connect offline, you should definitely do that. But a smaller, lower-pressure first step is a coffee date via an old-fashioned phone call.

Online connections and social media are incredible, but when we keep them only online, we miss out on human connection — which beats internet connection any day. Social media can create a false sense of intimacy. Sure, you can watch your friends' Instagram stories to help her pick out a dress for date night. And you can pour a glass of wine and settle in on the couch to keep up with how your friend's home renovation projects are going. But all of those points of connection are missing some human elements.

Although it's not quite true that 93 percent of our communication is nonverbal, things like vocal tone and facial expressions play an undeniable role in our ability to connect with the women in our lives.[5] A 2009 study revealed that there are situations where our facial expressions communicate things that we simply can't express in words alone (spoken or typed).[6] Empathy is most often communicated in nonverbal ways, especially our facial expressions, to let the other woman know that she's listened to, known, and loved. As women, we use a huge variety of nonverbal behaviors to express empathy and closeness with friends. We rely on these nonverbal cues more than men, and we're also more likely than men to pick up on these nonverbal signals.[7]

Our vocal tone is also lost when we only communicate with someone via text. More than likely, we can all remember a time when we misinterpreted a text message just because we assumed the wrong tone. Our vocal intensity and tone can help the woman who is listening to us determine our levels of emotions like depression, anger, and politeness.[8] So as much as a text or email makes a good starting point, we're not going to get the full picture of how our friend is *really* doing unless we transition away from a digital-only friendship.

"Friendships, in particular, have a natural decay rate in the absence of contact, and social media may well function to slow down the rate of decay. However, that alone may not be sufficient to prevent friendships eventually dying naturally if they are not occasionally reinforced by face-to-face interaction," writes Robin Dunbar, a professor of psychology.[9] After 2020, I think many of us are well aware of the beauty and gift of Zoom calls, Facetime chats, and phone calls. This real-time interaction is so valuable because it is a gift of our true presence. It wasn't just a passing comment made on a friend's post in the middle of the afternoon. Instead, it was carving out space to interact with people face-to-face, even if through a screen. When we lived through a season where those were our main tools of communication, things like vocal tone and facial expression became worth their weight in gold.

I'll never forget when a friend I'd connected with online shared that she was struggling with the same things I was in a season of mothering little babies. We chatted for over an hour, swapping mom hacks and laughs, but also feeling an incredible sense of being known by the other. Babies chattered in the background, coffee cups clinked on table tops, and the laundry machine whirred as we talked. We were both in the same season of life, and even if we were time zones apart, we knew we weren't alone in the joys, struggles, crosses, and triumphs of working motherhood.

If picking up the phone seems like an intimidating first step, start even smaller. I've loved using voice apps like Telegram, Discord, and Marco Polo to connect with friends using voice messages and short videos! Being able to see facial expressions and hear vocal tones, even if it's not in real time, can help you grow in your ability to give and receive sisterhood online!

Many times, we're tempted to take an all-or-nothing approach to the topic of digital friendship and even the way that we interact with our phones. Either we exist with our friends solely over on the 'gram, or we chuck our phones in the ocean and swear off any social media.

But as Catholic women who are striving for holy, wholesome, and authentic sisterhood, we need to stand somewhere in between living for private messages and fishing our phone out of the sea water. Digital friendship should include a healthy mix of communication both online and off, and the platforms on which we connect should be tools and gifts that we use, instead of letting them use us in an addictive way. I'm incredibly thankful for the friendships in my life that started because of a digital connection, and I pray that the digital connections in your life can blossom into full-fledged holy sisterhood.

Receiving the Gift of Digital Friendship

The next time a woman comments on your social media post or replies to your Instagram stories to share a laugh over a meme, ask her how her day is going and receive her story and her friendship.

Giving the Gift of Digital Friendship

Friends with a woman you connected with via Instagram, DM's, or in the comment section of a Facebook group? Invite her to a (digital) coffee date. Whether it's a phone call or a Zoom call, intentionally connect with her this week in real time.

with **Lea-Ann Virnig**

Friendships in Complicated Seasons

"**I** was accepted to the program," my husband quietly stated, not wanting the kids to overhear. We both knew what those words meant — another move was on the horizon. This program was a great move for his career; however, it hadn't been in our plan. When the surprise opportunity came up, we thought it was a long shot — so he applied. Getting this news changed our whole trajectory. Another move had not been in our plans! Two months earlier, my husband, an active-duty officer in the United States Air Force, had returned from a year-long deployment to Korea, and our family was still healing from the time of separation. Announcing to the kids that we were unexpectedly moving sent our family into a tailspin as we spent the next six months on the emotional roller-coaster of preparations for the inevitable.

I recall the day we walked through the door of the home my husband had found for us — although I thought I had prepared myself, the feelings of overwhelm engulfed me. This was our seventh cross-country move in our twenty years of marriage. When we were younger, and the kids were not yet teenagers, our moves held an excitement of seeing new places and meeting new people. Having done the homework before the move, I would jump in with both feet, playing the part of the supportive military wife. I knew just where to plug into community with other moms. Within weeks I was arranging playdates, attending mom's groups, hustling the kids to co-op classes, and volunteering at church. I'd prided myself on the smooth transitions we made.

This move was different — I was reeling from emotional scars left by a year of separation, family strife, and unhealthy friendships destroyed by competition and bitterness. On top of managing my emotional wounds, I was juggling concerns for my two broken-hearted teenage daughters, and battling fears that my college-aged boys wouldn't want to return home to a place they hadn't lived. All the while, I did my best not to squash my youngest two children's adventurous optimism. Smooth is not an adjective I would use to describe this move. I was being stretched in new ways and I lacked the control — or the illusion of it — that I had clung to in our other moves. I was feeling resentful, overwhelmed, and isolated.

I felt no desire to plug into a new community. I battled tears each time I came home from encountering new situations. The small talk required of the new relationships exhausted me! My extroverted nature had turned in on itself in self-pity. I went through the motions needed to sustain my family, but I erected walls around my heart, becoming numb to those around me. I was reluctant to invest myself in any budding friendship. Lies swirled in my head that the energy and vulnerability required to develop meaningful friendships wasn't worth it. I knew we wouldn't be here long, and I told myself I'd just manage on my own. It would be better that way. I found myself in a season where friendship seemed nearly impossible.

Donning the mask that life was fine, I assured everyone we were adjusting. My husband was super busy with his doctorate studies, being gone in classes all day and then studying late into the night. My loneliness grew, but I did my best to ignore it and threw myself into the school year.

But after months of trying to ignore the pain and fight off despair, I cracked. One day, while I was in the car by myself, I pulled off to the side of an isolated road crumbling into a heap of shaking sobs I cried out, "God, what am I supposed to do? I am so lonely! Where are you? Help me!" The floodgates opened, and his grace penetrated my heart. God reminded me, "Day by day, and grace by grace. Trust me." This was an inspiration he had given me while

Jon had been in Korea, and he once again called me to lean into his grace.

Father Jacques Philippe explains in *The Eight Doors of the Kingdom: Reflections on the Beatitudes,* "God sometimes allows it that we not find support from others in order that we find our comfort solely in him." God was drawing me deeper. I began pouring myself into prayer and reading, finding solace in my relationship with Christ. My dependence on the Blessed Mother became my lifeline as I sat at her feet and asked her to hold me close. The Eucharist became my daily companion as often as possible, giving me strength. Slowly the Lord revealed that he was with me in this solitude, and he had a purpose for it. In the quiet echoes of my lonely heart, I began to hear the comforting whispers of my Heavenly Father. Through his words in Scripture, he reminded me of the truth of his love and my identity, dispelling the lies that had begun to take hold of my heart that all the effort I put in wasn't worth it ... it was all pointless ... nobody would ever really understand me, or truly love me. Through reading and pondering both modern-day spiritual authors and the writings of Padre Pio, Saint Thérèse, and Saint Faustina, my prayer life deepened exponentially and I experienced a whole new depth of God's love.

As the roots of my faith and trust grew more robust, the Holy Spirit began revealing to me places in my heart he desired to heal, places where I had allowed wounds to fester and lies to take root, incrementally pushing out God's truth. Dr. Bob Schutchs, in the book *Be Healed,* explains that "Initially our distorted beliefs protect us from feeling pain, but in the long term, they become the mechanism by which our pain gets locked into our body and soul. These distorted beliefs become the building blocks that form the strongholds in our minds and hearts." I came face to face with layer after layer of my brokenness. With the aid of the Holy Spirit, my husband, and my spiritual director, I am working through these dark recesses, bringing them to God's healing light. I am a work in progress!

During this season, when friendship was so complicated, the Lord used my loneliness to bring me to my knees and reveal to me the strongholds that I had allowed to keep me from the depths of his love and the love of those around me. Slowly I am allowing the walls that I built up to come down, and the relationships in my life deepen as I share what the Lord is doing in my heart. Ever faithful, in time he brought new friendships into my life. Friendships built on a foundation of faith and honest sharing that I know will endure — even through the distance as we prepare to move again. Through this time, the Lord has revealed a new path that he is preparing me and calling me to walk in order to help other women seek healing as they grow in their relationship with him for, in the words of Father Jacques Philippe, "the consolation we receive from God is not for us to keep for ourselves. Rather, we in our turn are to become consolers of those who need it."

I would not have chosen this path on my own — and it has been watered with many tears. But through those tears God has cleared my vision and helped me to see a little more as he sees. Now, when I recognize the ache within, it no longer scares me, as I know if I enter into it the Lord will meet me there.

Lea-Ann Virnig, a writer and speaker passionate about inspiring women to live in the freedom of their identity in Christ, helps women cultivate their magnanimity and grow in holiness through wholeness. A revert to the Catholic faith, she has homeschooled for 16+ years, holds a certification in Youth Ministry, and is completing certification as a spiritual director through Divine Mercy University. Lea-Ann is a military wife to Jon, her husband of 22 years, and together they are raising six beautiful children brought to them through birth and adoption. You can find Lea-Ann on Instagram @leaann.virnig or her website TheMagnanimousLife.com.

9

When Friendship
Seems Impossible

I pray that this book on friendship has been just as much a balm to your soul to read as it has mine to write it; but I also know that you might have cracked open this book, read up to this chapter, and arrived at these last few pages feeling lonely and incredibly isolated. Diving deep into the topic of female friendship is beautiful, but it can also stir up an ache in your soul if you're living in a season or situation where friendship feels like an unattainable dream.

We've talked about striving for Eucharistic friendship, spoken into what authentic friendship truly means, and navigated through friendships in seasons of transition. Together we've had conversations about competition, comparison, and the gifts of hospitality and vulnerability. We've covered digital friendship and receiving the other. But maybe, just maybe, you've flipped through those conversations and topics wishing you could see yourself in these pages, but coming up short. Feeling alone, and perhaps more alone than ever. If every suggestion and story you've read so far in the past chapters has left you whispering, "But that won't work for me," this chapter is for you.

Maybe you work the night shift at a local hospital and you're trying to catch a few hours of sleep while most of your friends are hanging out, and you feel left out and alone. Or perhaps you're living in a rural community and it's particularly hard to connect with others. You might be fresh out of college and figuring out the minutiae of adult life, or maybe you're a recent transplant into a new city, and you're struggling to meet new people while missing the built-in community from a previous season. You may be serving in the military or be married to someone who is currently serving, which means you might have to pack up your home and move across the country (or the world!) at a minute's notice. This lack of stability can make forming friendships difficult to say the least.

If face-to-face friendship with other women isn't possible in this stage of your life, don't despair. Let's spend these last few pages together getting into the practicals of how to strive for sisterhood when that dream seems impossible. Remember that God is a good father who shows up and keeps his promises — and he has promised that he will never leave us orphaned.

Live in the Present Moment

Especially if you're in a difficult season, it can be easy to fall into the trap of spending most of your time wishing things looked different. You may wish you lived somewhere else, worked somewhere better, or that your life looked like anything but what it actually is. There's something important I want to tell you: Friendships can be found in the most unlikely of places, *if* you are truly living in the present moment. But you won't be able to receive the gift of that friendship if you're constantly looking around you for something else. You'll miss out on what's right in front of you in your search for anything different than your current reality.

"Every day you're alive, the future will stretch out before you, giving you something to anticipate, to think about, to focus on. And because it's an imaginary future, with no real sufferings or inconveniences in it, it will always be more attractive than the life you're living," writes Emily Stimpson Chapman in her book *Letter to Myself from the End of the World*. "This is why living for the future always breeds discontent with the present. A real imperfect present can never compare to an imagined perfect future." Your current situation might be far from what you'd imagined or hoped for. But it is the real, messy, present moment in which the Lord is inviting you to be truly rooted.

If night shifts are keeping you from a "normal" social life, ask the Lord if he's inviting you to grow in friendship with the women you see at work every night. If living in a rural area means that you can't see friends without hours in the car, God might be asking you to invest in friendship with an elderly neighbor or the clerk you see at the small-town grocery store every week. Or if you're hanging up your new diploma on the wall of your first post-college apartment, find your local parish and start going to Mass there regularly. Make a point of getting out of your comfort zone and be the one to initiate conversation. Don't wait on someone to notice that you're new — take initiative and start to give the gift of friendship to the women you find in the pews beside you. If you just moved to a new city, find a new place to do an activity you love doing. If you love Pilates, turn off the YouTube video workout and find a local gym where you can take a class alongside other women. Or if your hobby of choice involves crafting and creating, search for a local knitting or painting group. Bonding over the familiarity of a shared passion or hobby can help break the ice with someone new.

It's also important to keep in mind that you don't have to set out to make thirty new friends or recreate the exact friend group you had in the last season of life you were in. You can just start with one friendship, investing your time with one other woman. Starting small gives you a few actionable steps you can take, which can squash any analysis paralysis you may experience around new friendships and where to start. Start small and be open.

God is good at surprises, and he is present in the present moment. If you're longing for connection in this season, ask him to lead you to an unexpected friend. Ask him for the grace to be receptive to an unexpected, unconventional friendship!

Become a Regular at Your Favorite Local Spot

Find a favorite place in your new surroundings to become a regular at — find your spot! Maybe you can create a new routine of always going to the same place for Saturday morning breakfast, or always going to the same Mass time at your local parish. Perhaps your Friday evenings can end with a relaxing cup of tea at a local bookstore. In my current season, that means going to the library at the same time each week with my daughters, which means we get to chat with the same librarians, and share the play area with the same moms and their little kids. When I spend time away from the home and recharge so that I can come back and love my husband and kids better, I go to the same adoration chapel at the same time every Monday night. This has given me the chance to get to know the people who have the adoration hour before and after me. We exchange whispered hellos and prayer requests, and we kneel beside each other in adoration of Jesus in the Eucharist.

When you create a routine, you'll begin to start seeing the same people. Maybe it's the woman who sits behind you at Mass, or the volunteer coordinator who arranges the schedule at a place where you're tithing your time. Don't be afraid to be the first one to initiate a conversation. If you're an introvert like I am, this could be a push out of your comfort zone. Remember, you already have something in common with someone — you share a love of the same coffee shop or you're both members at the same parish. This commonality becomes an immediate conversation-starter. And, if you lean more to the extroverted side of things, you've probably already started those conversations on your own.

Whether it's speaking to your regular grocery clerk by name and asking how her day really was, or getting to know the bartender at your Friday night spot, invest in the other regulars who congregate at your new favorite spot and get to know them through your mutual interests. These women might not be in the same season of life as you. But becoming a regular at a local spot can create opportunities to dismantle an echo chamber and enter into friendships with women who don't look, act, or live exactly like you. They could be older than you, or decades younger. They might work while you stay at home with littles. These women might pray differently, rest differently, or raise their kids in a totally different way than you would. But soul-sharing friendship isn't limited to the woman whose life looks exactly like yours, so be open to the beauty of sisterhood that defies your expectations.

Getting to Know the Heavenly Sisterhood

Despite being alone physically, you are never alone spiritually. There are countless women in the heavenly sisterhood who want to be friends with you.

"Therefore, since we are surrounded by so great a cloud of witnesses, let us also lay aside every weight, and sin which clings so closely, and let us run with perseverance the race that is set before us, looking to Jesus the pioneer and perfecter of faith," Saint Paul encouraged his readers in his Letter to the Hebrews (see 12:1–2). This cloud of witnesses is composed of all who have gone before us into heaven — family members, friends, martyrs, and countless women throughout the entire history of the Catholic Church. Each and every one is cheering you on. Not only do they desire your joy in Christ, they also can't wait for you to join them in their unending song of praise in heaven. Talk about a holy and authentic community!

But making friends with these saints can feel a bit foreign — after all, you can't really invite Servant of God Dorothy Day over for a movie night (she'd probably vote for rewatching Super Woman for the thousandth time) or meet up with St. Teresa of Ávila for appetizers after work (she'd definitely order the spicy wings). And it's important to note that while every saint-friend can absolutely lead us closer to Christ through her example, writings, and intercession, there are also some aspects of the lives of the saints that we're not called to imitate in our daily lives today. For instance, the Lord is not calling us to ditch healthy eating habits in favor of eating only the Eucharist for nourishment like St. Catherine of Siena did for the last few years of her life, or lock ourselves in our room like St. Julian of Norwich. But every saint can lead us closer to Christ and help us become the women he created us to be. Despite the years (centuries!) separating us, friendship with the saints can be an incredible consolation during times where sisterhood on earth seems impossible. Work late hours? That's okay, the saints don't have a bedtime. Live far away from everyone you love, or find yourself constantly moving around? These women aren't bound by space or time.

But what does heavenly friendship look like practically? We can actually learn a lot about friendship *with* the saints *from* the saints. For instance, in 1887, St. Thérèse of Lisieux went on pilgrimage to Rome and visited the tomb of Saint Cecilia. There she learned about the life of the early Christian martyr, and began to form a friendship with her.

Thérèse remembered the trip to Rome in her autobiography, *A Story of a Soul*, writing, "Before my trip to Rome I didn't have any special devotion to this saint, but when I visited her house transformed into a church, the site of her martyrdom, when learning that she was proclaimed patroness of music not because of her beautiful voice or her talent for music, but in memory of the virginal song she sang to her heavenly Spouse hidden in the depths of her heart, I felt more than devotion for her; it was the real tenderness of a friend. She became my saint of predilection, my intimate confidante." She later wrote a poem originally titled "The Melody of Saint Cecilia" for her sister Celine's twenty-fifth birthday.

Friendship with a saint can begin with spending some time learning about their life. It could start with a quick internet search or reading through a devotional based on lives of the saints like *No Unlikely Saints*, a devotional series created and published by Brick House in the City, or *Pray for Us: 75 Saints Who Sinned, Suffered, and Struggled on Their Way to Holiness*, a fantastic collection of quick saint stories curated by Meg Hunter-Kilmer that I've loved reading recently. She introduced me to many of the saints that I'll share with you in this chapter!

Often, our friendships with the saints can seem a little one-sided. Saints who lived centuries ago can seem out of touch with your current reality. And this one-sided feeling isn't helped by the fact that the saints in heaven don't need anything from us. They don't need our encouragement to live holy lives themselves because they've already attained the ultimate goal of heaven.

But once you discover some shared experiences with the saints, conversation with them can seem more natural. For instance, St. Jane de Chantal struggled with depression, which can make her the perfect person to talk to if you're experiencing a darker season of life. St. Elizabeth Ann Seton was a mother, so she's a great saint to reach out to if the trenches of motherhood seem overwhelming, or if you just need someone to share a joy in the present moment of parenting your kids. But regardless of which saint you get to know, every single woman in the heavenly cloud of witnesses wants to lead you closer to Christ. She wants to cheer you on in your daily life because she ultimately wants to get to know you face-to-face in heaven. Meeting the saintly women who we've befriended here on earth (or who have befriended us!) will be such a joyful reunion in the life to come.

If you're open to a heavenly friendship, these women may find you before you find them. Some of my dearest friendships with the women in heaven weren't initiated by me! St. Catherine of Siena found me as I stumbled through her writings in a small devotional book. Meanwhile, Our Lady of Guadalupe surprised me with her friendship that started when she and I were re-introduced through a holy card from a friend. Don't be afraid to ask the Lord specifically to introduce you to some new saint friends.

The sheer number of women in heaven can be overwhelming, and you'll undoubtedly find one to accompany you through any season of life or situation.

If you're a single Catholic woman, you could grow in friendship with Blessed Consuelo Aguiar-Mella Díaz (1898–1936). She was a Uruguayan woman who lived in Spain during the Spanish Civil War. At thirty-eight, she was a working woman in a dating relationship with a man from Spain before she was martyred for her Catholic faith. Another amazing woman is St. Zita of Lucca (1212–72), a single Catholic woman who was so diligent to her work as a domestic servant that the family who employed her eventually put her in charge of their entire household.

You might be in a season of discernment, asking the Lord if he's calling you to religious life. Some holy women to walk beside you include household names like St. Thérèse of Lisieux (1873–97), who discerned a call to the Carmelite order when she was only fifteen. Despite the fact that she spent her entire adult life in a cloistered convent, she is the patron saint of missionaries because of her unceasing prayer for missions around the world. A lesser-known saint who also was called to religious life is St. Dulce Pontes (1914–92), who took vows with the Missionary Sisters of the Immaculate Conception of the Mother of God. She was a Brazilian sister who started schools, ministered to the homeless, and was nominated for a Nobel Prize!

Or maybe you're engaged and not only planning a wedding

but also preparing for marriage. A saintly woman who has been there and done that is St. Marie-Azélie Guérin Martin (1831–77), a successful lacemaker who married her husband, Saint Louis, after a three-month courtship. The couple would go on to have many children together, including St. Thérèse of Lisieux!

Maybe you're a married woman but you don't have any children of your own — you can get to know Servant of God Elisabeth Leseur (1866–1914). Elisabeth was married to her husband Felix, an atheist journalist and diplomat. After she converted to Catholicism, she wrote down her prayers and desires for her husband to join her in the Faith. The couple didn't have any children together, but Elisabeth dedicated herself to the creation of affordable housing for young working women. Despite his ridicule, she faithfully prayed for and loved Felix. It wasn't until reading through her journals after her death that Felix saw the beauty of Catholicism and later became a Dominican priest.

Perhaps you're in the trenches of young motherhood. If you're slathered in spit-up and unsure what day it is because you were up all night with a crying baby, Blessed Maria Quattrocchi (1884–1965) is a woman who knew all too well the discomforts that often accompany young motherhood. She gave birth to three children in four years, and wrote to her husband about her worries about taking care of young children when she was so exhausted. As her children got older, Maria wrote articles and books about parenting and spoke to women's small groups about family life. The Lord called two of her sons to the priesthood, and her oldest daughter to consecrated life.

Saints are real people, too, and many of them have gone through the same sticky situations we find ourselves in today. For instance, if you're going through a breakup, you could grow in friendship and solidarity with Venerable Gertrude van Oosten (1310–58), a Dutch woman whose fiancé left her for another woman. Gertrude went on to befriend the woman her ex-fiancé ended up marrying.

You might be facing infertility, which can make friendship with women like St. Agatha Yi Sosa (1784–1839) invaluable. After only three years of marriage, her husband passed away. Despite longing for children of her own, she never remarried or became a biological mother. She instead focused on intentionally loving her little brother, who was almost twenty years younger than her. Or if you're navigating the grief of losing a child to miscarriage or stillbirth, friendship with St. Gianna Molla (1922–62) can be a great comfort. She and her husband Pietro lost their fourth and fifth children to miscarriage.

You might be trying to find some semblance of order in your life as a Catholic working mom, juggling work hours and babysitters, dinner plans and deadlines. Blessed Eurosia Fabris Barban (1866–1932) was a mother to fourteen who also was a successful dressmaker and seamstress. At her dressmaking shop, she intentionally accompanied the women who worked for her, sharing the beauty of the Catholic Faith with them. On the flipside, you might be a stay-at-home mom, working through the never-ending pile of laundry between playdates and bath times. Saint Anne, the mother of the Blessed Mother, is a beautiful companion for the long days at home with littles.

Maybe you're in the second half of life as a Catholic woman. Your kids may have flown the nest, leaving you with free time to explore your passions and desires to serve others in new ways. St. Frances of Rome (1384–1440) was an Italian noblewoman with a great love of ministering to the poor of Rome. After focusing on raising her children in the Faith and tragically losing both her son and daughter to a plague, Frances established a community of women who didn't take vows, but simply dedicated themselves to prayer and ministry with the poor. She didn't live in the community house, though. She stayed at home with her husband until he later passed away. Then, she spent the rest of her life serving in the streets of Rome.

There also might be saintly women already in your life who you can get to know better. Perhaps you already have a confirmation or patron saint who you can grow more intimate with. I chose Saint Cecilia as my confirmation saint back in eighth grade. She and I regularly visit while I play piano at home all these years later. I also count St. Maria Goretti (whose feast day is one day before my birthday!) as one of my dear heavenly friends, and I love celebrating her life in the month of July with a novena that leads up to her feast day. You can also explore the lives of the saints through different books about the lives of the saints, or even books that they've written themselves (Saint Thérèse's *Story of a Soul* and *Essays on Woman* by St. Teresa Benedicta of the Cross come to mind).

Remember that just like it takes intentional time, good conversation, and healthy vulnerability to build friendships with women here on earth, the same is also true for these holy women. Don't be afraid to pray to them daily to intercede and get to know them better through conversation and their witness during their time on earth.

Growing in Relationship with Our Lady

While certain saints are great friends for particular seasons in our lives as women, Our Lady offers the perfect friendship for all of us as Catholic women today. Regardless of whether we're single, consecrated, married, or mothering, Mary longs to befriend each and every one of us and draw us closer to her son.

At first glance, Mary might seem a little out of reach as a friend. She never sinned, after all. She didn't lose her temper at Joseph or Jesus after a long day in that little house in Nazareth. She always said "yes" to God — in the big things he asked of her, like bearing Christ made flesh in her womb, and in the small moments of the hidden years we don't even see recorded in Scripture. But instead of seeing Mary as a woman who has everything together and is perfectly unrelatable, the first step to growing in relationship with

Our Lady is recognizing she was (and is!) *human.*

She was a young girl, engaged to be married and wondering about the plans God had for her life. She was the bride of Joseph, navigating parenting decisions together with him as they raised Christ. She was a mom, and although she might not have lost her temper with Jesus, she did lose him in the temple for three days. Our Lady had friendships with other women that she intentionally fostered, like her relationship with her older cousin, Elizabeth. She wasn't afraid to make bold asks in her prayer, like when she spurred Jesus on to start his public ministry at the wedding at Cana because the bride and groom had run out of wine. Then, Mary suffered immense pain as she gazed up into the eyes of her son as he hung on the cross, unable to do anything but simply exist with him in that moment.

But in that moment on the cross, Christ gave us the gift of himself and the gift of feminine friendship and maternal care from his own mother. "When Jesus saw his mother, and the disciple whom he loved standing near, he said to his mother, 'Woman, behold, your son!' Then he said to the disciple, 'Behold, your mother!' And from that hour the disciple took her to his own home" (Jn 19:26–27). Christ wants each and every one of us to take Mary into our own homes and our own hearts. Not to look at her and roll our eyes at her unattainable perfection, but to be reminded of what life fully alive as a Catholic woman looks like.

"The Church sees in Mary the highest expression of the 'feminine genius' and she finds in her a source of constant inspiration," John Paul II explains in his *Letter to Women.* Our Lady always said yes to the Lord, and she wants to walk alongside us as our mother and as our friend, encouraging us to offer our own *fiat,* our own yes.

I grew particularly close to Our Lady when I was preparing for the Sacrament of Marriage. The summer before our wedding, I nannied for a local family. Each afternoon, I'd load their little girl in a stroller and we'd go on a walk until she fell asleep. I invited Mary to come with us on those long walks. I entered into imaginative prayer while I pushed the stroller along, thinking about what it would be like to walk alongside Mary, chasing after an exploring toddler Jesus. These days, I'm in my own season of motherhood and I've found great comfort and friendship with Our Lady from being able to just invite her along with me during the day. I know she washed dishes, folded laundry, and cooked for her family — all daily tasks that I enter into, too. I ask her to come along for the ride and help me learn how to love and encounter Christ in the little moments with my family. Mary has helped me learn that the long days of parenting little kids aren't a reason to skip over prayer because of busyness or sheer exhaustion. Instead, this is the season of life where I can learn to make those seemingly mundane tasks like diaper changes or dishwasher unloading into a prayer themselves. Those (rare!) quiet moments in my day are where she invites me to ponder the goodness of God in my own heart, just like she did.

You might be in a different season of life, but I know Our Lady will accompany you in your day-to-day tasks if you invite her along! If you'd like to make things official in your friendship with Our Lady, one way to do this is by consecrating yourself to her.

Just what is Marian consecration? "Consecrating ourselves to Mary means accepting her help to offer ourselves and the whole of mankind to him who is holy, infinitely holy; it means accepting her help — by having recourse to her motherly heart, which beneath the cross was opened to love for every human being, for the whole world — in order to offer the world, the individual human being, mankind as a whole, and all the nations to him who is infinitely holy," John Paul II explained on May 13, 1982.

If you're interested in learning more about the practicals of Marian consecration, I'd recommend Father Michael Gaitley's book, *33 Days to Morning Glory: A Do-It-Yourself Retreat in Preparation for Marian Consecration.* In his book, Father Gaitley takes the principles of St. Louis de Montfort and presents them in layman's terms. You'll spend thirty-three days praying with short reflections on four huge Marian saints — St. John Paul, St. Louis de Montfort, St. Maximilian Kolbe, and St. Teresa of Calcutta. Then, at the end of your preparation, you'll pray a simple prayer consecrating yourself to Jesus through Our Lady. I loved getting to know Our Lady better as a mother and a friend through the preparation in Father Gaitley's book, and it's a beautiful place to also encounter the lives of the saints who were impacted by their relationship with the Blessed Mother.

Holy and authentic friendship with women is friendship centered on Christ — and there's no woman better equipped to journey alongside you as a Eucharistic friend than Our Lady. Regardless of whether you're surrounded by friends or finding sisterhood challenging or nearly impossible, there is never a bad time to grow in friendship with Our Lady. She's the perfect Eucharistic friend and model for holiness in our daily lives as Catholic women.

Receiving the Gift of Friendship in Seemingly Impossible Circumstances

This week in prayer, ask the Lord specifically to introduce you to a new friend in the heavenly sisterhood. God has a fantastic gift of matching us up with new friends from among the mystical body of Christ, and this request isn't a prayer he says no to. Then, be on the lookout for a new saint to get to know and grow in friendship with!

Giving the Gift of Friendship in Seemingly Impossible Circumstances

Is this a season that Christ is inviting you to lean into him and discover authentic friendship in him? Whenever you feel particularly lonely this week, as you long for the friendship in your life to look different, offer that ache up for someone specific. This might be a friend from a past season of life, or someone you know who is suffering.

Conclusion

We value good, holy, and authentic friendships because these relationships here on earth point us back to Christ. No matter what season of life you're in the middle of, and even (especially) if friendship feels totally impossible, Christ is inviting you into a deeper intimacy with him than ever before. And sister, I can say this with confidence, without even knowing the particulars about the place and season you find yourself in.

Why? Because Christ desires friendship with you.

Does this kind of intimacy with the Creator of the universe sound radical — even scandalous! — to say? We have Christ's very word to prove it. "No longer do I call you servants, for the servant does not know what his master is doing; but I have called you friends, for all that I have heard from my Father I have made known to you," John's Gospel tells us. "You did not choose me, but I chose you and appointed you that you should go and bear fruit and that your fruit should abide; so that whatever you ask the Father in my name, he may give it to you" (15:15–16).

Right now, you may not know exactly what God is doing in

your life. You may have found yourself questioning his plan, and on the hardest of days wondering if he even has one.

But Christ calls you friend. God wants to live his divine life in and through you. He hasn't and will never abandon you. In fact, just the opposite. Jesus desires to accompany you and tell you everything he hears from the Father. And this isn't a friendship that you're trying to force, as if Christ is a reluctant friend, someone who has to spend time with you out of some sort of obligation. No! *Christ chose you.* He wants you to live a life that bears fruit that lasts forever, even into eternal life. He wants you to ask for what you need.

Jesus wants to be even closer to you than your closest friend — closer than your best friend is even capable of. He wants to hear you, anytime of the day. You don't have to wait for a good time to talk to him, or figure out exactly how to say what you feel. He knows your heart better than you do. He desires to speak with you, through Scripture and time in conversation and prayer. He wants to spend every moment of the day with you, and he will never feel as if he's had enough time with you. On the cross, he became totally vulnerable with you, and he desires to receive the gift of your authentic vulnerability in return. He thirsts for you.

Throughout this book, we've defined what makes someone a good friend: someone who is honest, loyal, vulnerable, trustworthy, and hospitable. Good friends encourage you, desire you to grow into the woman God created you to be, and support you when your cross is heavy. But I think that we can sum up a good friend by asking how much she reminds us — by word or action — of the constant love and intimacy of Christ.

Spend time with the person who defines friendship, with God who is love itself. Love isn't something that God does, it's the defining characteristic of who he is. And he loves you. He wants to be near to you. He wants to be intimate with you and show you what true friendship means.

I don't know all of the exact details of the situation you find yourself in, but I know one thing for sure: Christ is the fulfillment of every desire we have for relationship and friendship, and he is inviting you to take a step closer to his Sacred Heart. He longs to show you the beauty of true, Eucharistic friendship. He stands at the door of your heart, knowing everything you are going through at this exact moment, and he knocks.

Will you say yes to his invitation of divine intimacy and friendship?

Notes

Introduction

1. "The 'Loneliness Epidemic,'" U.S. Health Resources & Services Administration, January 10, 2019, https://www.hrsa.gov/enews/past-issues/2019/january-17/loneliness-epidemic.

2. "New Cigna Study Reveals Loneliness at Epidemic Levels in America," MultiVu, Accessed October 20, 2021, https://www.multivu.com/players/English/8294451-cigna-us-loneliness-survey/.

3. Kira Asatryan, "Surprising Differences between Lonely Women and Lonely Men," *Psych Central*, November 26, 2015, https://psychcentral.com/blog/surprising-differences-between-lonely-women-and-lonely-men.

4. Ibid.

5. "Gendered Communication: Differences in Communication Styles." Point Park University Online, May 27, 2021, https://online.pointpark.edu/public-relations-and-advertising/gender-differences-communication-styles.

6. Kristin Fuller, "The Importance of Female Friendships among Women," *Psychology Today*, August 16, 2018, https://www.psychologytoday.com/us/blog/happiness-is-state-mind/201808/the-importance-female-friendships-among-women.

7. John Paul II, *Mulieris Dignitatem*, August 15, 1988, accessed October 21, 2021, https://www.vatican.va/content/john-paul-ii/en/apost_letters/1988/documents/hf_jp-ii_apl_19880815_mulieris-dignitatem.html.

Chapter 1

1. John Paul II, "General Audience, 16 January 1980 — the Human Person Becomes a Gift in the Freedom of Love," accessed October 20, 2021,

https://www.vatican.va/content/john-paul-ii/en/audiences/1980/documents
/hf_jp-ii_aud_19800116.html.

2. Shelley E. Taylor, Laura Cousino Klein, Brian P. Lewis, Tara L. Grue-
newald, Reagan A.R. Gurung, and John A. Updegraff, "Biobehavioral Responses to Stress in Females: Tend-and-Befriend, Not Fight-or-Flight," *Psychological
Review*, (July, 2000), https://taylorlab.psych.ucla.edu/wp-content/uploads
/sites/5/2014/10/2000_Biobehavioral-responses-to-stress-in-females_tend-and
-befriend.pdf.

3. "The Sacrament of Penance and Reconciliation," *Catechism of the Catholic Church*, accessed October 30, 2021, http://www.scborromeo.org/ccc
/p2s2c2a4.htm.

4. Ibid.

5. "Forgiveness: Your Health Depends on It," Johns Hopkins Medicine,
accessed October 20, 2021. https://www.hopkinsmedicine.org/health
/wellness-and-prevention/forgiveness-your-health-depends-on-it.

6. "The Theology of the Body by John Paul II," accessed October 30, 2021,
https://d2y1pz2y630308.cloudfront.net/2232/documents/2016/9/theology_of
_the_body.pdf.

Chapter 2

1. C. S. Lewis, *Mere Christianity* (London: William Collins, 2017).

2. Alice von Hildebrand, "Love and Friendship," *Catholic News Agency*,
August 19, 2016, https://www.catholicnewsagency.com/column/53596/love-and
-friendship.

3. Ibid.

4. Teresa of Calcutta, *No Greater Love*, ed. Becky Benante and Joseph Dure-
pos (Novato, CA: New World Library, 2002).

Chapter 3

1. Peg O'Connor "When to End a Friendship and How to Do It." *Psychology
Today*, July 17, 2017, https://www.psychologytoday.com/us/blog
/philosophy-stirred-not-shaken/201707/when-end-friendship-and-how-do-it.

2. Aristotle, Nichomachean Ethics, trans. W. D. Ross (The Internet Classics
Archive), http://classics.mit.edu/Aristotle/nicomachaen.html.

3. "Sympathy (n.)," Etymonline, accessed October 20, 2021, https://www
.etymonline.com/word/sympathy.

4. von Hildebrand, "The Gift of Friendship," *Catholic News Agency*, accessed October 20, 2021, https://www.catholicnewsagency.com/column/53416
/the-gift-of-friendship.

5. Ellie Lisitsa, "'Sliding Door' Moments," What Makes Love Last (blog),
The Gottman Institute, August 10, 2012, https://www.gottman.com/blog
/what-makes-love-last-sliding-door-moments.

6. Greg J. Stephens, Lauren J. Silbert, and Uri Hasson, "Speaker–Listener Neural Coupling Underlies Successful Communication," *National Academy of Sciences*, Proceedings of the National Academy of Sciences — PNAS 126, no. 32 (2010): 14425-14430, https://doi.org/10.1073/pnas.1008662107.

7. von Hildebrand, "Love and Friendship," Catholic News Agency, accessed October 20, 2021, https://www.catholicnewsagency.com/column/53596 /love-and-friendship.

8. von Hildebrand, "The Canons of Friendship," *Catholic Culture*, accessed October 20, 2021, https://www.catholicculture.org/culture/library/view .cfm?recnum=7125.

9. von Hildebrand, "Love and Friendship," *Catholic News Agency*, accessed October 20, 2021, https://www.catholicnewsagency.com/column/53596 /love-and-friendship.

10. Ibid.

11. Brené Brown, "Brené Brown on Boundaries," YouTube, accessed October 20, 2021, https://www.youtube.com/watch?v=6YiUhWSl_Q4.

12. John Cloud and Henry Townsend, *Boundaries: When to Say Yes, How to Say No to Take Control of Your Life,* (Harpercollins Christian Pub, 2017).

13. Carly Breit, "Why Ending a Friendship Can Be Worse than a Breakup." *Time*, September 24, 2018, https://time.com/5402304/friendship -breakups-worse-romantic/.

14. Gretchen Rubin, "Happiness Myth No. 3 — Venting Anger Relieves It," March 4, 2009. https://gretchenrubin.com/2009/03/happiness-myth-no-3 -venting-anger-relieves-it/.

Chapter 4

1. Andrew Francis-Tan and Hugo M. Mialon,"'A Diamond Is Forever' and Other Fairy Tales: The Relationship between Wedding Expenses and Marriage Duration," *SSRN*, September 15, 2014, https://papers.ssrn.com/sol3/papers .cfm?abstract_id=2501480.

2.Caryle Murphy, "Half of U.S. Adults Raised Catholic Have Left the Church at Some Point," Pew Research Center, September 15, 2015, https://www .pewresearch.org/fact-tank/2015/09/15/half-of-u-s-adults-raised-catholic -have-left-the-church-at-some-point/.

3. Edith Stein, "Principles of Women's Education," 'Kolbe's Greatest Books of World Civilization, August 14, 1999, https://www.kolbefoundation.org /gbookswebsite/studentlibrary/greatestbooks/aaabooks/stein /principleswomeneducation.html.

Chapter 5

1. "Survey Finds Constantly Checking Electronic Devices Linked to Significant Stress," American Psychological Association, February 23, 2017, https://

www.apa.org/news/press/releases/2017/02/checking-devices.

2. "The Facebook Effect: How Is Social Media Impacting Your Stress Levels?," *Health E-Living Blog* (blog), Chester County Hospital, March 12, 2020, https://www.chestercountyhospital.org/news/health-eliving-blog/2020/march/how-is-social-media-impacting-your-stress-levels.

3. Flic Taylor, "Hit 'Unfollow' on Social Media to Improve Your Mental Health," *Snapclarity* (blog), *Medium*, February 20, 2019, https://medium.com/snapclarity/hit-unfollow-on-social-media-to-improve-your-mental-health-b7d5e73bba3b.

4. Fr. David Vincent Meconi, *Christ Alive in Me: Living as a Member of the Mystical Body* (Steubenville, OH: Emmaus Road Publishing, 2021).

5. Meg Jay, *The Defining Decade: Why Your Twenties Matter and How to Make the Most of Them Now* (New York: Twelve, 2021).

6. Kristin Layous and Sonja Lyubomirsky, "How Do Simple Positive Activities Increase Well-Being?," *SAGE Journals* (February 2013), https://journals.sagepub.com/doi/abs/10.1177/0963721412469809.

Chapter 6

1. Edith Stein, "Principles of Women's Education Saint Edith Stein." Kolbe's Greatest Books of World Civilization, accessed November 13, 2021, http://www.kolbefoundation.org/gbookswebsite/studentlibrary/greatestbooks/aaabooks/stein/principleswomeneducation.html.

2. Rebecca Harris, "The Loneliness Epidemic: We're More Connected Than Ever - But Are We Feeling More Alone?," *The Independent*, March 30, 2015, https://www.independent.co.uk/life-style/health-and-families/features/loneliness-epidemic-more-connected-ever-feeling-more-alone-10143206.html.

3. Margaret Brady, "Tend and Befriend: How Female Friendship Helps with Healing," *Verily*, June 11, 2019, https://verilymag.com/2019/06/tend-and-befriend-how-female-friendships-help-with-healing-girlfriends-2019.

4. Pope Francis, Angelus, July 17, 2016, https://www.vatican.va/content/francesco/en/angelus/2016/documents/papa-francesco_angelus_20160717.html.

5. Fr. David Vincent Meconi, *Christ Alive in Me: Living as a Member of the Mystical Body* (Steubenville, OH: Emmaus Road Publishing, 2021).

Chapter 7

1. Barbara Markway, "Brené Brown's Netflix Special Busts Six Vulnerability Myths," *Psychology Today*, May 13, 2019, https://www.psychologytoday.com/us/blog/shyness-is-nice/201905/bren-browns-netflix-special-busts-six-vulnerability-myths.

2. Brady, "Tend and Befriend," *Verily*, June 11, 2019.

Chapter 8

1. R. I. M. Dunbar, "Do Online Social Media Cut through the Constraints That Limit the Size of Offline Social Networks?," *Royal Society Open Science*, January 1, 2016, https://royalsocietypublishing.org/doi/full/10.1098/rsos.150292.

2. Suzanne Degges-White, "Are Online Friends Better than No Friends at All?," *Psychology Today*, October 5, 2018, https://www.psychologytoday.com/us/blog/lifetime-connections/201810/are-online-friends-better-no-friends-all.

3. Jeffrey A. Hall, "How Many Hours Does It Take to Make a Friend?," *Journal of Social and Personal Relationships* 36, no. 4 (2019): 1278-1296, https://doi.org/10.1177/0265407518761225.

4. Tiffany Young, "Peanut - the Matchmaking App for Modern Motherhood: The Journey to 100m Profile Views," *Forbes Magazine*, November 19, 2018, https://www.forbes.com/sites/tiffanyyoung1/2018/11/19/peanut-the-matchmaking-app-for-modern-motherhood-the-journey-to-100m-profile-views/.

5. Jeff Thompson, "Is Nonverbal Communication a Numbers Game?," *Psychology Today*, September 30, 2011, https://www.psychologytoday.com/us/blog/beyond-words/201109/is-nonverbal-communication-numbers-game.

6. Chris Frith, "Role of Facial Expressions in Social Interactions," *Philosophical Transactions of the Royal Society B: Biological Sciences*, 364, no. 1535 (2009): 3453-3458, https://doi.org/10.1098/rstb.2009.0142.

7. Ann Neville Miller, "Men and Women's Communication Is Different—Sometimes," *Communication Currents (blog), National Communication Association*, February 1, 2011, https://www.natcom.org/communication-currents/men-and-women%E2%80%99s-communication—sometimes.

8. Norman N. Markel, Monte F. Bien, and Judith A. Philips, "The Relationship Between Words and Tone-of-Voice," *Language and Speech* 16, no. 1 (1973): 15-21, https://doi.org/10.1177/002383097301600102;

Nalini Ambady and Debi Laplante, "On How Things Are Said: Voice Tone, Voice Intensity, Verbal Content, and Perceptions of Politeness," *Journal of Language and Social Psychology* 12, no. 22 (2003): 434-441, https://doi.org/10.1177/0261927X03258084.

9. Dunbar, "Do Online Social Media Cut Through the Constraints That Limit the Size of Offline Social Networks?"

About the Author

C<small>HLOE</small> L<small>ANGR</small> is the host of the *Letters to Women* podcast. A Catholic Book Award Winner, she is also the author of several books including *Created for Love: Reflections for the Catholic Bride-to-Be* (OSV, 2019) and *Letters to Women: Embracing the Feminine Genius in Everyday Life* (TAN Books, 2021). She lives in the heart of the Midwest with her husband, Joseph, and their two daughters. She's frequently found drinking espresso, reading a mystery novel, or trying in vain to keep her houseplants alive. Discover more of her work online at LetterstoWomenPodcast.com.